COMBAT LEGEND

F-4
PHANTOM

Martin Bowman

Airlife

Text written by Martin W. Bowman
Profile illustrations created by Dave Windle
Cover painting by Jim Brown – The Art of Aviation Co. Ltd

First published in the UK in 2003
by Airlife Publishing, an imprint of The Crowood Press Ltd

British Library Cataloguing-in-Publication Data
A catalogue record for this book
is available from the British Library

ISBN 1 84037 401 2

Printed in Malaysia

*Contact us for a free catalogue that describes the complete range of Airlife
books for pilots and aviation enthusiasts*

Airlife Publishing

An imprint of The Crowood Press Ltd
Ramsbury, Marlborough, Wiltshire SN8 2HR
E-mail: enquiries@crowood.com
Website: www.crowood.com

Contents

F-4 Phantom II Timeline

27 May 1958
YF4H-1 BuNo. 142259 flies for the first time, at Lambert Field, St Louis.

27 March 1961
First production F-4B flies for the first time at St Louis.

November 1963
First USAF F-4Cs enter service.

5 August 1964
First F-4 combat sorties of Vietnam War.

12 March 1965
First RF-4B flies at St Louis.

9 April 1965
First F-4 air combat victory – over a Chinese MiG-17.

October 1965
First Phantom fighters arrive in Europe (81st TFW at RAF Bentwaters).

7 December 1965
F-4D version first flown.

27 May 1966
First flight of production F-4J.

21 February 1967
2,000th Phantom II (an F-4D for the USAF) delivered.

30 June 1967
First F-4E flies.

29 April 1968
Phantoms enter service with the Royal Navy.

23 August 1968
Phantoms enter service with the RAF.

September 1968
3,000th Phantom (an F-4J for the USN) delivered.

1 February 1971
4,000th Phantom (an F-4E for the USAF) delivered.

1971
First deliveries of RF-4Es to the *Luftwaffe*.

June 1973 to April 1976
175 two-seat F-4Fs built for the *Luftwaffe*.

24 May 1978
5,000th Phantom II (an F-4E for Turkey) delivered.

25 October 1979
5,057th and last McDonnell Douglas-built Phantom (an F-4E for Korea) delivered.

20 May 1981
Last Japanese-built F-4EJ delivered.

Late 1982
MoD announces that a new Squadron (No. 74) is to be formed using refurbished USN F-4J Phantoms.

August 1984
First three F-4Js for the RAF flown to the UK.

August to December 1990
Operation *Desert Shield*. Alabama ANG deployed with six RF-4C aircraft.

January 1991
Operation *Desert Storm*. RF-4Cs fly day tactical reconnaissance missions. Some 48 F-4G Wild Weasels drawn from George AFB, California, and Spangdahlem AB, Germany, fly more than 2,800 sorties from Sheikh Isa, Bahrain. Following the Gulf War F-4Gs of the 52nd TFW assigned to Operation *Southern Watch* to patrol the no-fly zone over southern Iraq on lethal SEAD missions in conjunction with Wild Weasel HARM-equipped F-16C/Ds.

1. Prototypes and Development: YF4H-1 to RF-4C

Despite being designed as a specialised carrierborne aircraft, the Phantom was to become the most widely used American supersonic fighter during the era of the Mach-2, missile-launching fighter. No fewer than 1,264 F-4s were delivered to the US Navy (USN) and 2,640 to the USAF. Only the F-86 Sabre/FJ Fury exceeded the F-4 Phantom in numbers produced, but in terms of longevity, the North American design had a shorter career span than the Phantom. James S. McDonnell's plant at St Louis, Missouri, had made a name for itself since the late 1940s with a succession of carrier-based jet fighters for the US Navy. These began with the FD-1 (later FH-1) Phantom, followed by the F2H Banshee, which was used extensively in the

The original mock-up of the AH-1, pictured in May 1954, shows the single-seat cockpit, and flat wing and tailplane configuration. *(McDonnell Douglas)*

The revised mock-up of the F4H, with provision for J79 engines and four Sparrow missiles. *(McDonnell Douglas)*

Korean War, and the less successful F3H Demon. The Air Force too bought large numbers of McDonnell aircraft, in the form of the F-101 Voodoo long-range fighter and its RF-101 reconnaissance derivative. In 1953, however, McDonnell Aircraft Corporation suffered a severe setback when a fighter contract for the US Navy went to Vought and its F8U Crusader.

In August 1953, at its own expense, McDonnell began a series of evolutionary studies (Model 98) in an attempt to prolong the production life of the single-seat F3H Demon by the installation of more powerful engines, and expanding its range and all-weather capability. Design Chief Herman D. Barkey and his team produced five proposals known as the Model 98A–E, all of which were based on the F3H Demon and were to be powered by various engines. The Model 98A (F3H-E) would be powered by two Wright J67 turbojets and capable of Mach 1.69 at altitude. The Model 98B (F3H-G/-H) would be powered by two Wright J65s or two General Electric J79s; and be capable of Mach 1.52 and Mach 1.97,

respectively. The delta-winged Model 98C and the straight winged 98D, which also had a lengthened fuselage, would be powered by two Wright J65s or a pair of J79-GE-X207A turbojets. Lastly, the Model 98E (F3H-J) was designed with a larger and thinner delta wing. Easily exchangeable single- and two-seat nose sections were included to enable the Model 98 to fulfil a variety of roles. Further versatility was added by giving the forward fuselage the capacity to house alternatively the APQ-50 search radar, a missile fire-control system, mapping radar, cameras, or electronic reconnaissance equipment, in addition to four 20-mm cannon or retractable packs for 56 2-in (5-cm) FFARs (folding-fin aircraft rockets). Various external stores – bombs, rocket pods, nuclear weapons, missiles, and/or fuel tanks – could be carried on eight underwing stations and one beneath the fuselage.

In June 1957 McDonnell invited the Air Force to study its Model 98AD proposal for a two-seat USAF interceptor version. All carrier equipment was omitted and it was to be armed with four GAR-2 or GAR-4 Falcon air-to-air missiles (AAMs). However, the Air Force was not at this time prepared to consider versions of an aircraft designed initially to meet Navy requirements.

Therefore, the Model 98AD (like the Models 98DA and 98DB, respectively proposed as two-seat and single-seat ground attack aircraft armed with 20-mm M61A1 cannon) was not put into production. Neither at first was the Model 98P photographic-reconnaissance version because the USN already had a supersonic reconnaissance aircraft in the Vought F8U-1P Crusader. (This aircraft, however, lacked a night reconnaissance capability, which was being incorporated early in 1962 in the design of the RF-110A for the Air Force. It was not until February 1963 that the US Marine Corps

Bureau of Aeronautics Number (BuNo.) 142259, the first YF4H-1, is shown in the final assembly shop during May 1958. In the background are F-101 Voodoos (with the high-set tailplanes) and F3H Demons. *(McDonnell Douglas)*

(USMC) obtained authorisation to order the first nine of an eventual 46 RF-4Bs). Although initially there was no interest from overseas for export variants of the Model 98 (Model 98BB for the Royal Canadian Air Force in May 1959, Models 98BH and BJ for the *Luftwaffe* in October 1959, and the Model 98CJ for the RAF in June

YF4H-1 142259, pictured during taxiing trials at St Louis on 22 May 1958. It was powered by 41.36-kN (9,300-lb st) dry thrust, 65.82-kN (14,800 lb st) afterburning thrust General Electric J79-GE-3A turbojets. Sparrow mock-ups have been added and the main landing gear fairings and D-doors have been removed.

Below: YF4H-1 BuNo 142259, piloted by Robert C. Little, lands back at Lambert Field, St Louis, after a successful first flight on 27 May 1958. (both McDonnell Douglas)

1960), export markets eventually opened up. In 1964 the UK became the first overseas Phantom customer and other countries followed, boosting total F-4 production to 5,195 aircraft, with a peak production rate of two aircraft a day being reached in 1967–68.

Some Demon, some Banshee

The strongest contender to emerge from the Model 98 series was the F3H-G. It was a combination of a shortened Demon and a swept-wing Banshee, with straight tailplanes and the innovative 'coke-bottle' fuselage shape favoured in supersonic aircraft design. On 19 September

1953 McDonnell submitted an unsolicited proposal to the Bureau of Aeronautics (BuAer) for the single-seat, all-weather fighter, even though no requirement had yet been identified by the Navy. In mid-1953 the Grumman XF9F-9 and Vought XF8U-1, which had already been ordered, appeared to meet the Navy's requirement for supersonic fighters but the BuAer and the Deputy Chief of Naval Operations (CNO) encouraged McDonnell to submit a proposal for a single-seat, twin-engined, all-weather attack aircraft in competition with designs being submitted by Grumman and North American. In spring 1954,

McDonnell management authorised the building of a full-size F3H-G mock-up and in August a formal development proposal was submitted. In September the USN told McDonnell that its proposal was 'too vague' and asked the company to resubmit it. On 18 October the Navy issued a Letter of Intent (LoI) covering the planned procurement of two YAH-1 cannon-armed, single-seat attack aircraft prototypes (the AH-1 designation more accurately reflected the aircraft's ground attack mission) and a static test aircraft.

On 14 May 1955 the CNO requested a review of the AH-1 programme and it seemed that further development would be curtailed. Twelve days later, the BuAer requested that the two McDonnell prototypes (142259 and 142260) be completed as two-seat YF4H-1s (the second seat being occupied by a radar intercept officer (RIO). The pilot and RIO were seated in tandem under separate clamshell canopies with the top line of the RIO's canopy initially being flush with the top of the fuselage. The aircraft's primary role was all-weather fleet defence. Secondarily, it had to be able to operate in the air-to-ground role and was capable of carrying up to 7258 kg (16,000 lb) of bombs, rockets, and other ordnance on four underwing and one centreline stations. For the strike role, provision was made for the external carriage of a single special weapon. External tanks could be carried on the centreline station and the inboard wing stations to boost usable fuel load from the 7408 litres

(1,957 US gal) carried in six fuselage and two wing tanks to a maximum of 12480 litres (3,297 US gal). A retractable probe was fitted in the forward starboard fuselage to permit in-flight refuelling. No provision was to be made for guns so the YF4H-1, which would be armed only with four Sparrow III semi-active radar homing (SARH) missiles semi-submerged beneath the fuselage, became the first all-missile American fighter. A proposal for a folding-fin variant of the Sidewinder AAM was soon abandoned, as was provision for four 20-mm cannon. The aircraft had to have a two-hour patrol endurance at a distance of 250 nm (463 km; 288 miles) from the carrier and be able to remain airborne for two deck cycles (over three hours) without air-to-air refuelling (AAR). The aircraft was still planned around a wing with a quarter-chord sweep of 45° and constant anhedral. Power was to be provided by two 46.03-kN (10,350-lb st) dry thrust and 71.82-kN (16,150 lb st) afterburning thrust General Electric J79-GE-2 or -2A turbojets mounted in the lower portion of the fuselage.

Pre-production contract

On 25 July 1955 the Navy awarded McDonnell a contract to include not only the two previously ordered prototypes but also five pre-production

YF4H-1 BuNo. 142259, in the hands of test pilot Robert C. Little, was pictured during one of the aircraft's early test flights in June 1958 over the Mississippi River. *(McDonnell Douglas)*

aircraft (143388/143392). Almost simultaneously, the Navy contracted a competing design by Vought for two prototypes of the single-seat, single-engined, missile-armed F8U-3. Late in November 1955 the Navy inspected the YF4H-1 mock-up. Numerous design changes had to be made when extensive wind tunnel testing, completed in August 1956, revealed that the YF4H would encounter serious stability problems and be limited to speeds below Mach 2. These changes resulted in the 45° swept wing having a 12° dihedral on the folding outer wing panels, a dog-toothed wing leading-edge, a 23° anhedral on the one-piece slab tailplane (stabilator), and variable-area engine intakes with flat ramps to shear away the boundary layer from the forward fuselage. All of this delayed the initial structural release, which was not authorised until 31 December 1956. (On 19 December McDonnell had received an order for 16 more F4H-ls (145307/145317 and 146817/146821). No fewer than 1,500 subcontractors and suppliers from 28 states were involved in the project by this time. However, delays experienced with the J79-GE-8 engines led to

F4H-1 BuNo. 143391, the fourth development aircraft and the sixth F4H-1 built, undergoing land catapult trials prior to the carrier suitability programme. Note that the Sparrow missiles have their fins omitted to avoid damage from the catapult strop. *(McDonnell Douglas)*

their substitution in the first YF4H-1 of two 69.37-kN (15,600-lb st) thrust YJ79-GE-3 engines loaned from USAF stocks so that trials could begin in earnest.

The scheduled first flight of the YF4H-1 was moved from February 1958 to December 1957 and then back to March 1958 when it became known that the first flight would not now take place at Lambert Field in St Louis, but at Edwards AFB. Then, in September 1957, the BuAer changed the venue to St Louis once again and directed that the first flight take place in April 1958! As it turned out, the first flight took place on 27 May 1958, when 142259 was flown by chief test pilot Robert C. Little at Lambert Field, St Louis. It was not trouble free; the most serious problem being the loss of hydraulic power, which prevented the nose wheel from fully retracting. Despite the problems, Little landed safely. The second flight was also problematical and it was not until the third flight, on 31 May, that Little was able to go supersonic. (142259 was lost on 21 October 1959 during a maximum-altitude investigation flight, which killed its pilot Zeke Huelsbeck. The right engine aft access door was ripped off when Huelsbeck turned at Mach 2.15 over the California desert, causing the right engine to overheat and finally destruct).

The manufacturer's and Navy flight test evaluation that followed at the Naval Air Test

Center (NATC) at Patuxent River, Maryland, resulted in many changes being progressively incorporated into the overall design. The variable air intakes were modified by removing the upper lip extension and replacing the fixed splitter plates with a combination of variable (forward) and fixed (aft) ramps with bleed air holes on the fixed section, increasing the inlets from 12.7- x 20.3-cm to 25.4- x 35.6-cm (5- x 8-in to 10- x 14-in). The new intake configuration was first used in 145307, the sixth F4H-1F (later F-4A-2-MC). A revised radome provided space for a new radar and its larger dish, enabling the AN/APQ-50 radar and its 70-cm (24-in) diameter dish to be replaced (on 29 F4H-1s accepted from May 1960 to June 1961) by an AN/APQ-72 radar with a 86.4-cm (34-in) dish. Boundary-layer control through compressor air blown over the leading edge and trailing edge flaps was installed and was first tested on 143392, the fifth pre-production aircraft. An infra-red (IR) seeker was later added beneath the nose and a redesigned cockpit, with raised canopies to improve forward visibility for the pilot and increase headroom for the RIO, was also installed. Both the new radar installation and revised cockpit were first fitted to 146817, the 17th F4H-1F (F-4A-3-MC). Beginning with the 19th production machine, the F4H-1 would use J79-GE-8 engines.

Beating the Crusader III

In December 1958 the F4H-1 was declared the winner of the missile-armed, all-weather naval fighter competition against the Vought F8U-3 Crusader III and on 17 December McDonnell was awarded a follow-on contract for 24 F4H-1s (148252/148275). In March 1961, all 45 F4H-1 aircraft ordered before 17 December 1958 were re-designated F4H-1F (each aircraft being powered by two 73.38-kN (16,500-lb st) thrust J79-GE-2 or -2A engines) to differentiate them from later models powered by the J79-GE-8. On 3 July 1959 the F4H-1 was named Phantom II in a ceremony held at St Louis during the celebration of McDonnell's 20th anniversary.

(The roman numeral II was soon discontinued in popular usage because the FH-1 Phantom no longer remained in service by the time the Phantom II made its operational debut.) The F4H-1F aircraft were used for test and training, joining VF-121 'Pacemakers' in December 1960. Finally, on 18 September 1962, in accordance with the new Tri Service designation system, the F4H-1F became the F-4A. (The 144 J79-GE-8-powered F4H-1s, which were ordered in batches of 72 each, on 23 September 1959 and 1 August 1960, respectively, were redesignated as F-4B aircraft.)

From 15 to 20 February 1960, carrier suitability trials were undertaken using F4H-1 143391 aboard the USS *Independence* (CVA-62) off the Atlantic coast. On 15 February 143391, with Lt-Cdr Paul E. Spencer at the controls, made its first launch and recovery aboard the *Independence*. In all, some 18 catapult launches were made and the trials generally were very successful. From 25 to 27 April, further carrier trials were carried out aboard the smaller USS *Intrepid* (CV-11) and the 20 catapult launches and arrested landings were almost perfect. It was found, however, that the Phantom's arresting hook skipped once it touched the deck, but this problem was soon corrected. The engines proved very reliable, with wave-offs even being flown on one J79 and without using the afterburner. The trials revealed that the powerplant could be accelerated from approach power to full thrust in under a second. The heavier Phantom seemed to pose no problems for attack pilots more used to the lighter Douglas A4D Skyhawk, Grumman F11F Tiger and other types. Even though the Phantom weighed twice as much as the F11F and almost three times as much as a Skyhawk, its engine power was awesome, although it was heavy on fuel, especially if both afterburners were used. In July 1960 Board of Inspection and Survey (BIS) trials were carried out at NATC Patuxent River. By the end of the year two Replacement Air Groups (RAGs) were working up Phantom crews for fleet service. VF-121 received its first Phantom at Naval Air Station

These F-4Bs of VF-114 'Aardvarks' with Carrier Air Wing 11, intercepted this Soviet Tupolev Tu-16 'Badger' in the vicinity of the attack carrier USS *Kitty Hawk* (CVA-63) in the North Pacific Ocean in January 1963. *(USN)*

(NAS) Miramar, California, on 30 December 1960. On the East Coast, VF-101 'The Grim Reapers' also began equipping with the Phantom at Key West, Florida.

Production F-4B

On 27 March 1961 the first production F-4B (F4H-1), the most advanced free world fighter-interceptor of its day, destined to be the definitive original USN Phantom and the first to see combat, flew for the first time. The F-4B was powered by two 48.47-kN/75.60-kN (10,900 lb st/17,000 lb st) thrust J79-GE-8 turbojets and fitted with revised air intake ramps (the fixed ramp being set at 10° from the flight axis versus 5° on the modified F4H-1F intakes, and the variable ramp having a maximum setting of 14° versus 10°). It had APQ-72 radar with an 81.3-cm (32-in) diameter dish, a Lear

AJB-3 bombing system, folding wings and a tailhook. With the inboard wing pylons and the four semi-submerged well mountings under the fuselage combined, the Phantom could carry six 3.66-m (12-ft) long, 159-kg (350-lb) Raytheon AIM-7C Sparrow III SARH AAMs, although more commonly four Sparrows were carried, with four 2.83-m (9-ft 4-in) long, 70.3-kg (155-lb) Philco AIM-9B Sidewinder heat-seeking missiles carried on launch rails on the inboard wing pylons. The usable internal fuel load was increased slightly to 7506 litres (1,983 US gal). A total of 649 F-4B-6-MC to -28-MCs was delivered to the USN and USMC from June 1961 to March 1967; 29 of these being loaned to the USAF (62-12168/12196). Twelve F-4Bs were subsequently modified to F-4G standard, while three became YF-4Js and 228 were modified as F-4N machines. A handful was modified as DF-4B, EF-4B, NF-4B, or QF-4B Phantoms. As a result of combat experience in South-East Asia F-4Bs were progressively upgraded and modified. They received chaff dispensers, which were added above the rear fuselage sides and an electronic countermeasures (ECM) capability, which was continually upgraded. Most effective were the radar homing and warning system (RHAWS) and deception systems such as AN/ALQ-51 and AN/ALQ-100. A number of F-4Bs were also retrofitted with slotted stabilators, as fitted to the F-4J, to shorten take-off distance and reduce approach speed.

Into service

In July 1961, VF-74 'Bedevilers' and VF-114 'Aardvarks' began receiving Phantoms. They became the first two operational sea squadrons, going aboard the *Saratoga* (CVA-60) in the Atlantic, and the *Kitty Hawk* (CVA-63) in the Pacific, respectively. In June 1962, VF-96 'Fighting Falcons' became the second operational Pacific Phantom squadron and on 9 November that year was embarked in the USS *Ranger* (CVA-61). VF-102 'Diamondbacks' became the second operational Atlantic Phantom squadron and embarked in USS *Independence* (CVA-62) on 18 January 1962 for carquals (carrier qualifications) before making its shakedown cruise aboard the newly commissioned nuclear-powered USS *Enterprise* (CVAN-65). On 3 August *Enterprise*, with VF-102 on board, and the USS *Forrestal*, with VF-74 aboard, sailed from Norfolk, Virginia, for the Mediterranean. Meanwhile, in March 1962, VF-41 'Black Aces' completed its initial Phantom training and became the third operational squadron in the Atlantic Fleet on board the USS *Independence*. This squadron was deployed on temporary duty (TDY) to NAS Key West, Florida, on 9 October at the height of the tensions caused by the Cuban Missile Crisis.

By the end of the year two USMC squadrons – VMF(AW)-314 'Black Knights' and VMF(AW)-531 'Gray Ghosts' were operational, at Marine Corps Air Station (MCAS) El Toro, near San Diego, California, and MCAS Beaufort, South Carolina, respectively. '(AW)' indicated 'All-Weather'; this designation was dropped on 1 August 1963 when the F-4 became considered purely an interceptor. VMFA-513 'Flying Nightmares', a West Coast Douglas F-6A Skyray unit, became the third USMC squadron to receive Phantoms, early in 1963. In April that same year VMFA-314 deployed to Atsugi, Japan, and VMFA-351 joined it there in August, with VMFA-513 following in October. Together, they formed part of MAG 11 (Marine Aircraft Group 11) and they were joined finally by VMFA-542 'Bengals', in August 1965.

Reconnaissance RF-4B

The RF-4B reconnaissance version for the USMC (originally designated as the F4H-1P) first flew at

BuNo. 151975 was the first production RF-4B for the USMC and is pictured here during a pre-delivery flight on 12 March 1965. *(Richard Ward via Frank Mason)*

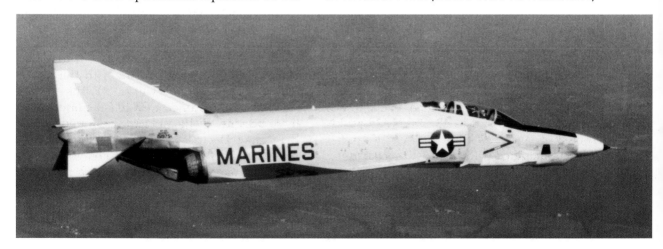

St Louis on 12 March 1965. A total of 46 RF-4Bs were built, the first 36 (151975/151983 and 153089/153115), retained the powerplant installation and much of the airframe of the F-4B, but the last ten (157342/157351) used the F-4J airframe and F-4B engines. All were fitted with an inertial navigation system and specialised electronic equipment in the nose and fuselage. Forward- and side-oblique cameras (or alternatively a mapping camera) were housed in a nose 1.42 m (4 ft 8 in) longer and also able to carry a SLAR (side-looking airborne radar) and IR sensors. Film could be developed in flight and the cassettes ejected at low altitude for rapid dissemination of aerial intelligence to ground commanders. For night photography, photoflash cartridges were ejected upward from each side of the aircraft.

RF-4Bs were first delivered to VMCJ-3 at MCAS El Toro, California, in May 1965 and soon after to VMCJ-2 at MCAS Cherry Point, North Carolina, and to VMCJ-1 at Iwakuni, Japan. In October 1965, VMCJ-1 flew its RF-4Bs to Da Nang for operations in Vietnam. During the war in South-East Asia three RF-4Bs were lost to anti-aircraft artillery (AAA) and small arms fire, and one in an operational accident. Deliveries of the RF-4B ended in December 1970. In 1975, two

This F-4C-22-MC, 64-0711, of the 12th TFW, is pictured over Vietnam early in the war. (USAF)

years after US combat operations in Vietnam had ceased, the RF-4Bs were regrouped in a new squadron, VMFP-3, and based at El Toro as part of the 3rd Marine Air Wing (MAW). In 1989, still attached to 3rd MAW, VMFP-3 was continuing to send RF-4B detachments wherever needed, to support not only its parent organisation, but also the 1st MAW in Japan, the 2nd MAW on the East Coast, and the 1st Marine Brigade in Hawaii. VMFP-3 stood down in August 1990.

Phantoms for the USAF

Although during the late 1950s the USAF had consistently refused to consider the Phantom for interceptor service, the political climate in the early 1960s forced it into a rethink. Newly appointed Secretary of Defense (SecDef) Robert S. McNamara sought to reduce defence expenditure by standardising as much of the armed forces' equipment as possible and he applied this doctrine to aircraft especially. In 1961 the USAF was therefore duty bound to reconsider the Phantom, first as a potential successor to the Convair F-106A Delta Dart interceptor in Air Defense Command (ADC), and later as a multi-role tactical fighter and tactical reconnaissance aircraft. During tests the F4H-1 proved that it could carry far heavier loads than the F-106A over longer distances, while having a 25 per cent greater radar range. It also required almost one-third less MMH/FH

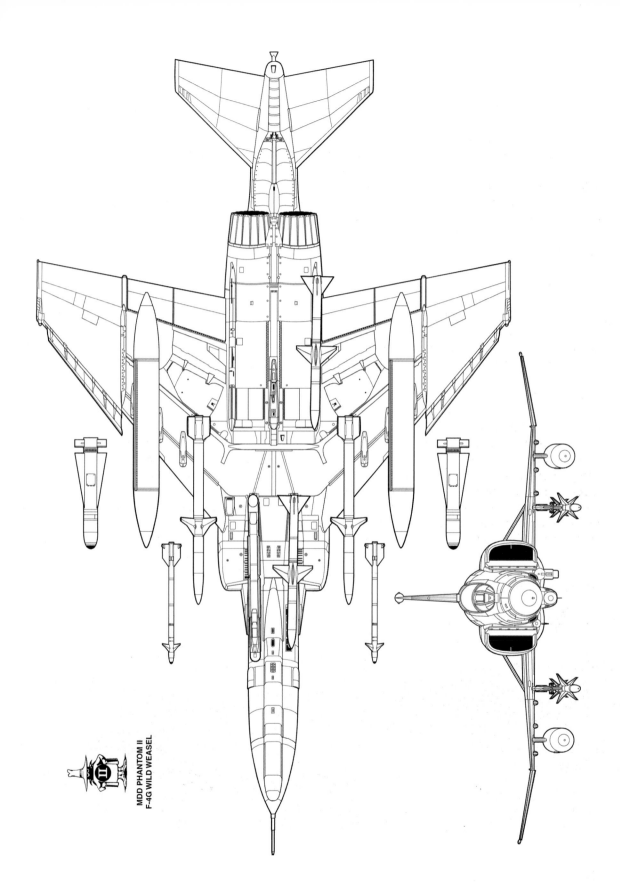

MDD PHANTOM II
F-4G WILD WEASEL

F-4B-14-MC 150482 (No.268) became YRF-4C (62-12201) for the USAF, as seen here at St Louis in March 1973. F-4B-14-MC 150480 was the first, and only other, YRF-4C (62-12200). *(McDonnell Douglas)*

(maintenance man-hours/flight hour). In the tactical fighter role too, the F4H-1F proved infinitely more versatile than the Republic F-105D Thunderchief, being able to carry air-to-ground ordnance while at the same time its lower wing- and power-loadings produced a much better all-round air superiority performance. True, the 'Thud' could carry a nuclear store internally and the Phantom could not, but this was no advantage because political thinking now was for less dependency on nuclear weapons, a 'conventional' response being favoured. The Phantom was also more suited to the tactical reconnaissance role than the RF-101C Voodoo, having a much better overall performance and, unlike the Voodoo, it could fly night photo-reconnaissance missions.

In January 1962, President John F. Kennedy requested Congressional approval for the procurement of tactical fighter (F-110A) and reconnaissance (RF-110A) derivatives of the F4H-1F for the USAF. On 17 January it was announced that 29 USN F-4Bs (F-110As) were to be transferred to the USAF (4453rd Combat Crew

Training Wing (CCTW) at MacDill AFB, Florida), to train instructor pilots before being returned to the Fleet. On 24 January McDonnell delivered two F4H-ls (149405 and 149406 – later receiving Air Force serials 62-12168 and 62-12169) to Langley AFB, Virginia, for evaluation by Tactical Air Command (TAC). On 30 March McDonnell received an LoI for one F-110A (62-12199), and a production contract for 310 F-4C aircraft soon followed. In April, the Department of Defense (DoD) announced that versions of the Phantom were to become the standard fighter and tactical reconnaissance aircraft of TAC, United States Air Force in Europe (USAFE) and the Pacific Air Force (PACAF), and on 29 May an LoI was issued for two YRF-110As (62-12200 and 62-12201). An order for 26 RF-110As (redesignated RF-4C on 18 September 1962) was authorised on 31 December 1962. The first F-4C flew on 27 May 1963 and the first of two YRF-4C prototypes (62-12200) made its maiden flight on 20 August that same year. The first F-4Cs became operational in the four squadrons of the 12th Tactical Fighter Wing (TFW) at MacDill AFB. The 8th TFW 'Wolfpack', the 35th TFW and the 366th TFW 'Gunfighters' followed it over the next three years. These four Wings later deployed ten Tactical Fighter Squadrons (TFSs) to South-East Asia in 1965–67.

2. Operational History: Phantoms in US Service

F-4B-14-MC BuNo. 150491 of VF-41 'Black Aces', is catapulted from the waist deck of the USS *Independence* (CVA-62) on 11 October 1965, in the Gulf of Tonkin. A pair of A-4s of VA-86 'Sidewinders' and a VA-72 'Blue Hawks' A-4E, prepare to launch from the bow cats. *(McDonnell Douglas)*

Including prototypes and development aircraft, 1,264 Phantoms were built for the USN and USMC and 2,840 were produced for the USAF.

US Navy service

In December 1960 F4H-lFs were delivered to VF-121, the Pacific Fleet RAG at NAS Miramar, California. Shortly after, Detachment A of VF-101, the Atlantic Fleet's RAG, also received F4H-lFs. In mid-1961 VF-74 and VF-114 became the first fully operational F4H-1F squadrons and in October that same year VF-74 became the first F4H-l squadron to complete carquals. The first short cruise was made from August to October 1962 by VF-102 'Diamondbacks' on board USS *Enterprise* (CVAN-65), while the first full deployment was made from August 1962 to

F-4B-13-MC BuNo. 150478/AG211, of VF-84 'Jolly Rogers', is catapulted from the waist deck of the USS *Independence* (CVA-62) on 11 October 1965, in the Gulf of Tonkin. *(McDonnell Douglas)*

March 1963 by VF-74 'Bedevilers' to the Mediterranean on board USS *Forrestal* (CVA-59). In March 1962, VF-41 'Black Aces' completed its initial F-4B training and became the third operational squadron in the Atlantic Fleet, on board the USS *Independence* (CVA-62). On 9 October 1962, during the Cuban Missile Crisis VF-41 was deployed on TDY from NAS Oceana, Virginia, to NAS Key West, Florida, with North American Air Defense Command, while F-4Bs operating from the *Enterprise* and *Independence* helped enforce the blockade of Cuba.

The war in Vietnam

At the time of the Gulf of Tonkin Incident on 2 August 1964, 13 of the 31 deployable Navy fighter squadrons were equipped with F-4Bs; one had a mix of F-4Bs and F-4Gs, and one was converting from F-3B Demons to F-4Bs. In addition, two RAG squadrons flew a mix of F-4As and F-4Bs. The first Phantom combat sorties were flown during Operation *Pierce Arrow* on 5 August,

Above: F-4Bs of VF-41 'Black Aces', A-4E Skyhawks of VA-86 'Sidewinders' and VA-72 'Blue Hawks', on board USS *Independence* (CVA-62) in the Gulf of Tonkin in October 1965.

Right: With everything down, F-4B BuNo. 151492 of VF-84 'Jolly Rogers' prepares to land on USS *Independence*. (both McDonnell Douglas)

when F-4Bs from VF-142 and VF-143 on board the USS *Constellation* (CVA-64) in the Gulf of Tonkin provided cover for retaliatory air strikes against North Vietnamese gunboats and shore facilities. Next to see action were F-4Bs from VF-92, VF-96, and VF-151, which flew combat air patrols (CAPs) during retaliatory strikes in February 1965 (*Flaming Dart*) and early *Rolling Thunder* raids in spring 1965. From August 1964 to August 1973, 22 Navy squadrons (and one Marine squadron) made 84 war cruises to the Gulf of Tonkin; 51 with F-4Bs, one with F-4Gs from 1965 to 1966, and 32 with F-4Js , the latter beginning with VF-33 and VF-102 aboard USS *America* (CVA-66) in May 1968.

The war cost 71 USN F-4s (five to enemy aircraft, 13 to surface-to-air missiles (SAMs), and 53 to AAA and small arms fire) in combat and 54 in operational accidents. At war's end, F-4s and Grumman F-14 Tomcats provided air cover during the final evacuation of South Vietnam in April 1975. F-l4As progressively replaced F-4Bs and F-4Js in most deployable squadrons except the six squadrons assigned to the older and smaller CVAs, USS *Midway*, *Franklin D. Roosevelt* and *Coral Sea*, which were eventually re-equipped with F-4N/S Phantoms. On 24 March 1986 VF-151 and VF-161, the last active duty carrier-based F-4 squadrons, were launched from *Midway* for the last time.

Naval Air Reserve

Phantoms first reached the Naval Air Reserve in 1969, when F-4Bs were assigned to VF-22L1 at NAS Los Alamitos, California. In 1970 four reserve fighter squadrons – VF-201 and VF-202

F-4B-26-MC 153018/NH-205, of VF-114 'Aardvarks', is seen flying from the USS *Kitty Hawk* (CVA-63) over the Gulf of Tonkin in March 1968. It is armed with Sparrows and Sidewinders. *(USN)*

with the Atlantic Fleet, and VF-301 and VF-302 with the Pacific Fleet – were established, but they were at first equipped with the Ling-Temco-Vought F-8 Crusader because active units urgently needed F-4s. In 1974, F-4Bs finally replaced the Crusaders and they were in turn replaced by F-4N and F-4S Phantoms. The last F-4N was flown by VF-201 from NAS Dallas, Texas, to Naval Air Technical Training Center (NATTC) Memphis, Tennessee on 29 February 1984. The last F-4S (155560) was retired by VF-202 at NAS Dallas on 14 May 1987. The Naval Air Test Center (NATC) and the Naval Test Pilot School (NTPS) operated F-4s at NAS Patuxent River in the period 1958–88. They also served in a wide range of experimental roles, mainly at NAS Point Mugu, NAS China Lake and NAF El Centro, California, NASWC/NWEC Kirtland AFB, New Mexico, and Naval Air Development Center (NADC) Johnsville, Pennsylvania.

Following the retirement of the last two F-4S Phantoms from the Strike Aircraft Test Directorate of the NATC, the only Phantoms remaining in USN service are F-4S aircraft at

NAS Point Mugu (with VX-4) and QF-4 drones at Pacific Missile Test Center (PMTC) Point Mugu and Naval Weapons Center (NWC) China Lake.

F4H-1/F-4B-11-MC 149457/VW-1 of VMF(AW)-314 'Black Knights', in flight in December 1962. (USMC)

US Marine Corps

In June 1962 VMF(AW)-314 'Black Knights' received its first F4H-ls at MCAS Cherry Point. By the summer of 1964, six squadrons were equipped with F-4B fighter-bombers (VMFA-115 and VMFA-323 at MCAS Cherry Point, VMFA-513 and VMFA-542 at MCAS El Toro, and VMFA-314 and VMFA-531 at Atsugi, Japan). Five others (VMFA-122, -212, -232, -324, -334) were about to convert from the F-8 Crusader to the Phantom. In May 1965, the RF-4B was first delivered to VMCJ-3 at MCAS El Toro and shortly thereafter to VMCJ-2 at MCAS Cherry Point and VMCJ-1 at Iwakuni in Japan. (In 1975 all RF-4Bs were absorbed into VMFP-3 at MCAS El Toro as part of the 3rd MAW. VMFP-3 finally stood down in August 1990.)

The first Marine Corps Phantoms to go to Vietnam were 15 F-4Bs of VMFA-531, which landed at Da Nang AB on 10 April 1965, flying their first combat sorties three days later. The F-4B was the only Marine aircraft that could carry two 2,000-lb (907-kg) bombs and proved well suited for the ground attack role in Vietnam, where, on average, loads of 2268 kg (5,000 lb) were carried. From 1965 to 1970 the 11 USMC F-4B squadrons operated on a rotational basis from Da Nang and Chu Lai in support of USMC ground forces in South Vietnam, and on *Tally Ho* offensive strikes in the North Vietnamese panhandle and *Steel Tiger/Tiger Hound* interdiction sorties in Laos. In-country Marine air operations continued at a high level during 1968–69 (now under Seventh Air Force control) but when US forces in Vietnam were reduced, units were progressively redeployed to Japan. VMFA-115, -212 and -232 returned to Da Nang in April 1972 following the North Vietnamese spring offensive and in May moved to Nam Phong, Thailand, to fly strikes against enemy LOCs (lines of communication) in Laos, and North Vietnam.

During the Vietnam War the Marines lost 72 F-4s in combat (one to a MiG, 65 to AAA and small arms fire, and six in mortar or sapper attacks on their bases) and 23 in operational accidents. At the end of the war, Phantoms remained the only fighter aircraft in service with the Marines until the arrival of the first McDonnell Douglas F/A-18 Hornets in January 1983. The last Marine F-4S machines were finally phased out early in 1989, the very last Marine Corps F-4 unit being VMFA-134 at MCAS El Toro, California, which received F/A-l8As in spring 1989.

F-4Bs were first delivered to the Marine Air Reserve in December 1973, VMFA-321 at NAF

Washington receiving the aircraft. The last Phantoms in reserve service were replaced by F/A-18s in 1990–91.

USAF

In November 1963 the first F-4Cs arrived with the 4453rd CCTW at MacDill AFB. In January 1964, F-4Cs began joining operational TAC units where they first replaced the 12th TFW's Republic F-84F Thunderstreaks. The first F-4Cs in the Pacific area were from the 555th TFS, which was assigned toTemporary Duty (TDY) with the 51st TFW at Naha AB, Okinawa, in December 1964.

Beginning in 1965, F-4Cs with 16- and 35-mm motion picture cameras were operated by the USAF to photograph the early flight phase of space projects. An F-4C was first used to photograph the launching of the moon-mapping Ranger capsule. (Later several manned space missions were recorded by Phantoms.)

In October 1965 the 81st TFW became the first unit to operate F-4C Phantoms in Europe when it arrived at RAF Bentwaters, Suffolk, England. Five months earlier, the 10th Tactical Reconnaissance Wing (TRW) at RAF Alconbury had received two RF-4Cs, the first

Six F-4Cs, carrying Sparrows and ECM pods, are led by a Douglas EB-66E ECM aircraft on the first radar-directed blind bombing mission of the Vietnam War, in 1965. Because the F-4 was not equipped for accurate medium level bomb delivery, Phantoms flew on bombing strikes in South-East Asia with a 'lead ship' which signalled when to release the bomb load. F-4C-20-MC 53-7640 was lost in Vietnam on 13 September 1968. *(McDonnell Douglas)*

An F-4E of the 526th TFS, attached to the 26th TRW, on the flight line at Takhli AB, Thailand on 15 April 1969. The 'E' was the only Phantom model built with internal gun armament. *(USAF)*

reconnaissance Phantoms assigned to a European-based USAF unit.

In April 1965 TAC F-4Cs of the 45th TFS, 15th TFW at MacDill AFB became the first Phantoms to see combat in South-East Asia when they deployed to Ubon Royal Thai Air Force Base (RTAFB), Thailand, on TDY assignment to the 2nd Air Division (AD). Initially, they were used to provide MiGCAPs (combat air patrols to protect attack aircraft from MiGs). On 20 June the first Phantom loss occurred when a 45th TFS F-4C was brought down by flak during a strike against barracks at Son La, North Vietnam. On 24 July an F-4C was brought down by a Soviet-built SA-2 'Guideline' SAM. (The SA-2 was a 10.67-m (35-ft) long, two-stage rocket with a 158-kg (349-lb) high-explosive warhead and a ceiling of almost 18288 m (60,000 ft). Pilots who encountered them described them as 'telegraph poles'.) In August the 45th TFS returned to the 15th TFW. On Christmas Day 1965, President Johnson suspended the *Rolling Thunder* bombing campaign to induce the Communists to negotiate. The Viet Cong (VC) responded with a counter-offensive campaign and *Rolling Thunder* was re-started on 31 January 1966.

By the end of 1965 there were 18 squadrons of 'fast movers' in South-East Asia, including six tactical fighter squadrons equipped with the F-4C. The 433rd and 497th TFS were based at Ubon RTAFB, the 390th TFS at Da Nang AB, and the 12th TFW's 43rd, 557th and 558th TFSs were based at Cam Rahn Bay AB. In March 1966, the 366th TFW arrived at Phang Rang AB with three squadrons of F-4Cs (moving to Da Nang AB in

F-4E-35-MC 67-0315/JV of the 469th TFS, 388th TFW based at Korat AB, Thailand, in May 1970. It is carrying bombs with detonators designed to ensure maximum blast effect. *(Frank Mason via Richard Ward)*

October). On 25 April the Mikoyan-Gurevich MiG-21 'Fishbed' was seen for the first time, and the following day two MiG-21s attacked three Phantoms escorting two Douglas RB-66 Destroyers. One of the F-4 pilots fired two Sidewinder missiles at one of the MiGs and the enemy pilot was seen to eject from the doomed fighter. The combat proved, as in Korea, that in

the hands of an accomplished pilot, a heavier machine could still beat a more manoeuvrable enemy fighter. On 14 July the first pair of MiG-21s were destroyed, by F-4Cs of the 480th TFS, 35th TFW. Of the 379 USAF aircraft lost in 1966, 42 were F-4Cs lost in combat and 14 were F-4Cs lost to operational causes. In 1967, some 17 MiG-21s were shot down by the USAF – 16 by the F-4Cs and one by a 433rd TFS, 8th TFW F-4D – for the loss of 95 F-4Cs and 23 RF-4Cs.

USAF F-4 crews mostly flew air-to-ground missions in South-East Asia, employing slick and retarded bombs with standard or extended fuses, rocket launchers, CBUs (Cluster Bomb Units) and BLU (Bomb Live Units) firebombs. At the end of May 1967 the 555th TFS 'Triple Nickel', 8th TFW at Ubon re-equipped with the F-4D and on 24 August the AGM-62A Walleye TV-guided missile was first used in combat, in a successful attack on a bridge. On 26 October, the 555th TFS first used an AIM-4 Falcon IR-guided missile to destroy a Mikoyan-Gurevich MiG-17 'Fresco'. However, disappointing results with the Falcon led to the 8th TFW modifying its F-4Ds to once again carry the USN-developed Sidewinder. On 25 May 1968, F-4Ds of the 8th TFW launched GBU-10 laser-guided bombs (LGBs) for the first time. In addition, F-4Ds of the 25th TFS seeded ADSID-1 (Air-Delivered Seismic Intrusion Device-1) seismic sensors along the Ho Chi Minh Trail and Mk 84 EOGBs (electro-optical guided bombs) were first dropped by Phantoms of the 8th TFW on 6 April 1972.

The Paul Doumer bridge

On 10 May 1972, the first day of the *Linebacker* campaign, the 8th TFW, using 'smart' (guided) bombs again, was tasked with the destruction of the massive 19-span, 1686 m (5,532 ft)-long Paul Doumer road and rail bridge, North Vietnam's premier transport target, on the outskirts of Hanoi. Several spans had been dropped by heavy bombing during *Rolling Thunder* in 1965 but later repaired, and in 1972 the bridge was once again a main artery linking North Vietnam and China. Sixteen Phantoms of the 388th TFW struck at marshalling yards at Yen Vien north of Hanoi using standard 500-lb (227-kg) bombs and 16 F-4Ds of the 8th TFW headed for the Paul Doumer bridge armed with 2,000-lb (907-kg) GBU-8 EOGBs. In the back seats of the Phantoms the weapon systems operators (WSOs) viewed the pictures produced by the TV cameras in the noses of each bomb and the contrast between light and shade on the target became the impact point. It seems that after release several of the bombs transferred lock-on from the bridge itself to the shadow of the bridge on the river, while others suffered guidance failures, because all of the EOGBs missed their target. The spans were finally brought down on 13 May 1972 by laser-guided 'smart' bombs dropped by F-4Ds of the 8th TFW.

By early 1968 there were 180 F-4Cs, RF-4Cs and F-4Ds in South-East Asia, of which about a quarter were RF-4Cs. RF-4Cs had first been assigned to the 33rd Tactical Reconnaissance Training Squadron (TRTS), a conversion unit at Shaw AFB, South Carolina, in September 1964 and shortly thereafter the 16th Tactical Reconnaissance Squadron (TRS) became the first operational RF-4C unit, at the same base. In South-East Asia the first RF-4Cs were nine aircraft of the 16th TRS, which were deployed on a TDY to Tan Son Nhut AB on 30 October 1965.

F-4E-35-MC 67-0309 of the 469th TFS, 388th TFW based at RTAFB Korat, pictured over North Vietnam in November 1970. *(McDonnell Douglas)*

The next day, combat operations began and during the next eight years RF-4Cs assigned at various times to the 11th, 12th, 14th, and 16th TRSs operated from Tan Son Nhut AB and Udorn RTAFB. No RF-4Cs were lost to MiGs but seven were shot down by SAMs, 65 were lost to AAA or small arms fire, four were destroyed on the ground, and seven were lost in operational accidents. (The RF-4C equipped 19 TRSs in TAC, PACAF and USAFE. By 1991 just three RF-4C squadrons (and six squadrons of the Air National Guard (ANG)) remained. By 1994 RF-4Cs equipped four units of the ANG only.)

Bombing halt

In November 1968 a bombing halt was imposed, which remained in force until 21 February 1972. During the halt, F-4s did not take part in offensive operations, flying only escort missions for reconnaissance aircraft over North Vietnam. In November 1968, the F-4E was assigned in-theatre when the 469th TFS at Korat RTAFB, Thailand, converted from the F-105D. When, in spring 1972, the North Vietnamese invaded South Vietnam, among the flood of units sent to Vietnam and Thailand on TDY as part of *Constant Guard* were 15 F-4 squadrons (seven with F-4Ds, six with F-4Es one with F-4Cs and one with EF-4C Wild Weasels). The first EF-4C Wild Weasel (defence suppression) Phantom finally entered service in June 1968 with the 66th Fighter Weapons Squadron (FWS), an operational conversion and tactics development unit based at Nellis AFB, Nevada. EF-4Cs went on to equip the 67th TFS at Kadena AB, Okinawa, which deployed on TDY to Korat RTAFB, Thailand, during 1972–73 for *Linebacker I* operations, and to the 81st TFS at Spangdahlem AB, West Germany.

Linebacker

Bombing of the North had finally resumed with a vengeance on 10 May 1972, with the *Linebacker I* offensive aimed at the enemy's road and rail system to prevent supplies reaching units in South Vietnam. *Linebacker II* operations began on

18 December 1972 and lasted until the 29th, with the USAF, USN and USMC carrying out an intensive aerial bombardment against industrial and communications targets, ports, supply depots and airfields in the Hanoi and Haiphong areas. USAF F-4Ds and F-4Es flew MiGCAPs as well as day- and night-escort missions for attack aircraft and Boeing B-52 Stratofortresses. During *Linebacker II* sorties, F-4Ds of the 555th TFS destroyed five enemy aircraft in the air. *Linebacker I* and *II* were the most effective offensives of the war (according to pilots who flew the missions, the North Vietnamese had 'nothing left to shoot at us as we flew over. It was like flying over New York City') and finally persuaded Hanoi to seek an end to the war. Although all US ground forces were withdrawn from South Vietnam, air raids into neighbouring Cambodia and Laos continued until August 1973. Both countries then fell to the Communists and the North turned its attentions to the final take-over of South Vietnam. On 15 August 1973, the last US combat missions in South-East Asia were flown. The USAF lost 442 F-4s (plus 83 RF-4Cs) – 33 were shot down by MiGs, 30 by SAMs and 307 by AAA and small arms fire. Nine were destroyed on the ground during mortar and sapper attacks and 63 went down as the result of operational incidents.

Post-Vietnam service

In 1975 the F-4 began to be supplemented by the McDonnell Douglas F-15 Eagle and in 1979, by the General Dynamics F-16 Fighting Falcon. Alaskan Air Command phased out its Phantoms in 1982 and USAFE's last F-4Es were those of the 52nd TFW at Spangdahlem AB, West Germany, which were replaced by F-16C/Ds in 1987. PACAF began phasing out its Phantoms in September 1981, when the 7th Air Force's 8th TFW at Kunsan AB traded its F-4Ds in for F-16s. Two squadrons of F-4Es were retained in the air defence role but began re-equipment with the F-16C/D from October 1988. The 36th TFS at Osan AB, South Korea, was the last USAF F-4 air defence unit when it traded in its last F-4Es for

F-16s early in 1989. The last US Phantoms in South-East Asia were the RF-4Cs of the 15th TRS at Kadena on Okinawa, which as a result of Fiscal Year 1991 (FY91) budget plans, relocated to Teagu AB and transferred the majority of its Phantoms to the Republic of Korea Air Force (RoKAF). Of the few USAF F-4 units remaining, in early December 1990 the 4th TFW at Seymour Johnson AFB, North Carolina, completed its conversion from the F-4E to the F-15E Eagle. By the end of 1992 the four squadrons of F-4Es and F-4Gs of the 35th TFW (which gained the aircraft when the 37th TFW was redesignated as a Lockheed F-117A Nighthawk unit) at George AFB, California, had gone.

The F-4G Advanced Wild Weasel version had entered operational service in 1978. In 1979 F-4Gs replaced the last EF-4Cs in service with active squadrons and the EF-4Cs were handed over to the 113th Fighter Squadron (FS), 181st Fighter Group (FG) and the 163rd FS, 122nd Fighter Wing (FW), of the Indiana ANG (where they were partially demodified and operated as F-4DCs). By 1990 F-4Gs were being operated alongside F-4Es by two squadrons of the 35th TFW at George AFB and alongside F-16C/Ds by one squadron of the 3rd TFW at Clark AB, in the Philippines. In Europe they equipped the 52nd TFW (alongside F-16C/Ds) in USAFE's 17th Air Force at Spangdahlem AB, West Germany.

Desert Storm Weasels
From 5 September to 26 December 1990, some 24 F-4Gs of the 52nd TFW deployed to Sheikh Isa, Bahrain, as part of the *Desert Shield* deployment to the Persian Gulf. On 16 January 1991 another 12 F-4Gs from the 52nd TFW were assigned to Incirlik AB, Turkey. During Operation *Desert Storm*, F-4G Wild Weasels drawn from the 81st TFS, 52nd TFW, and the 561st TFS, 35th TFW at George AFB, California, flew more than 2,800 sorties from Sheikh Isa, Bahrain, and Incirlik AB, Turkey. The F-4G's hunter-killer partnership with the F-16 proved so successful during the Gulf War that it led the USAF to retain a single squadron of F-4Gs – the 561st FS, formed in 1993 at Nellis AFB,

F-4D-28-MC 65-0699 of the 48th TFW at RAF Lakenheath, Suffolk. The 48th TFW received the remainder of its F-4D aircraft in September 1974. For two years the unit had averaged 26 Phantoms assigned, but finally reached its authorised complement of 72 during the July to September 1974 quarter. The wing was the last in USAFE to convert to F-4s, retaining them until 1976, when it began conversion to the F-111F. *(USAFE)*

Nevada – pending deployment of High-Speed Anti-Radiation Missile (HARM) Targeting System-equipped F-16s for use in conjunction with Boeing RC-135 Rivet Joint electronic warfare (EW) aircraft. Following the Gulf War the F-4Gs in the 52nd TFW were assigned to Operation *Southern Watch* and used to patrol the no-fly zone over southern Iraq on defence suppression/destruction missions in conjunction with Wild Weasel F-16C/Ds with interim AGM-88 HARM/AGM-45 Shrike capability.

Air Force Reserve (AFRES)
It was not until October 1980 that AFRES became a Phantom operator, when the 915th Airborne Early Warning and Control Group at Homestead AFB, Florida, was redesignated as the 915th Tactical Fighter Group (TFG) and F-4Cs were assigned to the 93rd TFS. By 1984, F-4Ds had been delivered to four more squadrons and the 93rd TFS had also been re-equipped with F-4Ds. In 1988 the 457th TFS at Carswell AFB, Texas, began receiving F-4Es and in 1989 the 93rd TFS became the first AFRES squadron to replace its Phantoms with F-16A/Bs. Conversion of the remaining four F-4 Phantom squadrons to F-16s was completed by 1991.

F-4E-32-MC 66-0336 of the 57th FIS 'Black Knights' at Keflavik, Iceland. *(USAFE)*

Air National Guard (ANG)

In February 1971 Phantoms were first assigned to the ANG when RF-4Cs were delivered to the 106th TRS, 117th TRG, Alabama ANG. Eight more ANG squadrons were equipped with the RF-4C and a replacement training unit, the 189th Tactical Reconnaissance Training Flight (TRTF) in the Idaho ANG operated from 1 September 1984 to late 1993. In January 1972 F-4Cs were first assigned to the 170th TFS, Illinois ANG and in 1977 F-4Ds first went to the 178th Fighter Interceptor Squadron (FIS). Two years later, recently redundant EF-4C Phantom Wild Weasels went to the 113th and 163rd TFSs, Indiana ANG. In 1985 F-4Es joined the ANG when the 110th TFS, Missouri ANG converted from F-4Cs. By early 1989 ANG units flying RF-4Cs had been reduced to five operational squadrons and one training squadron. As of 1 January 1991 the RF-4C was still in service with the 117th TRW at Birmingham, Alabama; the 124th Tactical Reconnaissance Group (TRG) at Boise, Idaho; the 152nd TRG at Reno, Nevada; the 155th TRG at Lincoln, Nebraska; the 163rd TRG at March AFB, California, and the 186th TRG at Meridian, Mississippi.

Desert Storm reconnaissance

During Operation *Desert Shield* the 106th TRS, 117th TRW, Alabama ANG deployed six RF-4Cs to Sheikh Isa, Bahrain, on a voluntary basis from August to December 1990. It was attached to the 35th TFW (Provisional) as the only RF-4C unit with LOROP (Long-Range Oblique Photography) capability. Using KS-127 66-in (1676-mm) focal length cameras, the RF-4Cs flew cross-border reconnaissance missions at stand-off ranges of up to 80 km (50 miles) before the start of hostilities. One RF-4C and its crew were lost during Operation *Desert Shield*, on 8 October. A second was lost after the end of Operation *Desert Storm* (by which time the Alabama ANG had been relieved by the 192nd TRS, 152nd TRG, Nevada ANG, which continued to fly the original RF-4Cs deployed). Attrition replacements were made with RF-4Cs of the Mississippi and Nevada ANGs. During *Desert Storm* RF-4Cs flew day tactical reconnaissance missions, which included search sorties for mobile 'Scud' missile launchers. By 1994 only the 117th Reconnaissance Wing (RW) and the 152nd, 155th, and 163rd Reconnaissance Groups (RGs) were still operating the RF-4C. By 1996 all had gone – the 117th, 155th and 163rd becoming Boeing KC-135 Stratotanker tanker wings and the 152nd a Lockheed C-130 Hercules airlift wing.

In 1991 the F-4E was still operated by the 108th TFW at McGuire AFB, New Jersey, the 122nd TFW at Fort Wayne, Indiana, the 131st TFW at St Louis, MO, and the 181st TFG at Terre Haute, Indiana. Three years later all these units had converted from the Phantom, leaving just the 124th FG at Boise, Idaho, with its F-4G Wild Weasels, which remained until the end of 1995.

3. The Phantom Men

From 1959 to 62 Phantoms set numerous speed, height and endurance records, including eight in 1962 alone.

6 December 1959: Project *Top Flight*. Cdr Lawrence E. Flint, Jr, USN, in a specially modified YF4H-1 (BuNo. 145311) climbed to 15240 m (50,000 ft) where he levelled off to accelerate before zooming to set a new absolute altitude record of 30,040m (98,557 ft) over Edwards AFB.

5 September 1960: Lt-Col Thomas H. Miller, USMC, flew F4H-1F (BuNo. 142260) over a 500-km (310.7-mile) triangular course in 15 minutes 19.2 seconds, at an average speed of 1958.16 km/h (1,216.74 mph).

YF4H-1 BuNo. 142259 is shown here with 'Project Top Flight' titles on its fuselage during training for the absolute altitude record attempt in December 1959. It has two Sparrows forward. *(McDonnell Douglas)*

25 September 1960: Cdr John Franklin (Jeff) Davis, USN, set a new record over the 100-km (62.1-mile) course in F4H-1 BuNo. 143389 at an average speed of 2237.41 km/h (1390.26 mph).

24 May 1961: Project *LANA*. For project *LANA* (L for the roman numeral 50 and ANA for the Anniversary of Naval Aviation), five F4H-lFs, competing for the Bendix Trophy, took off at timed intervals from Ontario, CA, and flew to NAS Brooklyn (Floyd Bennett Field), New York. In four supersonic dashes at altitudes of 15,240 m (50,000 ft), separated by three subsonic flight refuellings at 10,670m (35,100 ft) from tanker-configured Douglas A3D-2 Skywarriors, three of the Phantoms, flown by USN crews, reached New York having shattered the previous record (3 hours 8 minutes set in November 1957 by a USAF McDonnell RF-101C). The best time – for which the team of Lt Richard F. Gordon, pilot, and Lt (jg) Bobbie R. Young, RIO, of VF-121 received the Bendix Trophy – was 2 hours 47 minutes. This represented an average speed of 1400 km/h (870 mph) over the 3936-km (2,446-mile) flight.

28 August 1961: Project *Sageburner*. USN crew Lt Huntington Hardisty and RIO, Lt Earl H. 'Duke' DeEsch set a new low-altitude record over the 3-km (1.86-mile) course. Taking off from Holloman AFB, New Mexico, the crew flew

BuNo. 145307, *Sageburner*, of VF-101 Detachment A, pictured low over the Stallion Sight Valley in August 1961. *(McDonnell Douglas)*

twice in each direction at a maximum altitude of 38 m (125 ft) over rough terrain to average 1452.869 km/h (902.769 mph).

22 November 1961: Project *Skyburner*. In the second YF4H-1 (BuNo. 142260), which was specially fitted with a water/alcohol spray in the engine inlet ducts to cool the air ahead of the compressors and thus increase engine thrust, Lt-Col Robert B. 'Robbie' Robinson, USMC, flew twice over a 15/25-km (9.3/15.5-mile) course at Edwards AFB at an average speed of 2585.1 km/h (1,606.3 mph) at an altitude of 13715 m (45,000 ft), setting the world's first speed record at more than Mach 2.

5 December 1961: Using the Project *Skyburner* aircraft, Cdr G. W. Ellis, USN, set a new sustained altitude record of 20252.1 m (66,443.8 ft) from Edwards AFB.

21 February 1962: Project *High Jump*. Two time-to-height records were broken at NAS Brunswick, Maine, when Lt-Cdr John W. Young, USN, climbed to 3000 m (9,843 ft) in 34.52 seconds, and Cdr D. M. Longton, USN, climbed to 6000 m (19,685 ft) in 48.78 seconds.

1 March 1962: Project *High Jump*. Three time-to-height records were broken at NAS Brunswick: 9000 m (29,528 ft) in 61.62 seconds and 12000 m (39,370 ft) in 77.15 seconds by Lt-Col W. C. McGraw, USMC; and 15000 m (49,213 ft) in 114.54 seconds by Lt-Cdr D. W. Nordberg, USN.

31 March 1962: Project *High Jump*. Flying from NAS Point Mugu, CA, Lt-Cdr F. T. Brown, USN, climbed to 20000 m (65,617 ft) in 178.50 seconds.

3 April 1962: Project *High Jump*. Over NAS Point Mugu, Lt-Cdr John W. Young, USN, climbed to 25000 m (82,021 ft) in 230.44 seconds.

4 April 1962: Project *High Jump*. Lt-Cdr D. W. Nordberg, USN, set a new time-to-height record by climbing to 30000 m (98,425 ft) in 371.43 seconds. During the flight, Nordberg unofficially beat the 30,480-m (100,000-ft) record set by Cdr Lawrence E. Flint, Jr on 6 December 1959.

Things did not always go according to plan, however, and chasing records could be dangerous work. On 18 May 1961 Cdr J. L. Felsman, USN, flying 145316, the 17th aircraft built, suffered pitch dampener failure, leading to pilot-induced oscillation, which caused the aircraft to break up and explode while attempting to set a speed record at extremely low level at Kirtland AFB, New Mexico.

In combat over Vietnam

However, the Phantom men's greatest claim to fame was in the Vietnam War of 1965–73, where they became most famous for their MiG kills, ground-attack missions, suppression of enemy air defences (SEAD) sorties and attacks on bridges with 'dumb' and later 'smart' bombs. One of the bridge targets was the 165-m (540-ft) long, 17-m (56-ft) wide Ham Rong (Dragon's Jaw) road and rail bridge over the Song Ma River 5 km (3 miles) north of Thanh Hoa in North Vietnam's bloody Iron Triangle (Haiphong, Hanoi and Thanh Hoa), which stood 15 m (50 ft) above the river. It survived numerous hits from hundreds of Bullpup missiles and 750-lb (340-kg) bombs but refused to fall down. Almost 700 sorties were flown against the bridge at a cost of 104 crewmen shot down over an area of 194 km² (75 sq miles) around the Dragon. In March 1967, the USN attacked the bridge with Walleye guided bombs but failed to knock out the structure despite three direct hits. The spans were finally brought down three days into the *Linebacker* campaign on 13 May 1972 by LGBs dropped by F-4Ds of the 8th TFW. Unfortunately, by then the Communists had built several other back-up routes around the bridge and the flow of supplies across the Song Ma River was not seriously affected.

Phantoms and MiGs met each other over Vietnam on many occasions throughout the first half of 1967 and American crews also continued to run the gauntlet of SAMs and ground fire. The first F-4 air combat victory, which was not confirmed for fear of publicly antagonising the People's Republic of China, was made on 9 April 1965 when Lt (jg) Terence Murphy and Ensign Ron Fegan of VF-96 shot down a MiG-17 from China's Air Force of the People's Liberation Army. The Navy crew did not return to the USS *Ranger* (CVA-61), however; either they were shot down by a Chinese MiG-17 or mistakenly downed by another F-4B. The first officially confirmed USN victories over North Vietnamese fighters occurred on 17 June 1965. Cdr Louis C. Page, Jr, his RIO Lt John C. Smith, Jr and Lt Jack E. D. Batson, Jr and his RIO Lt-Cdr Robert B. Doremus of VF-21, flying from USS *Midway* (CVA-41), were vectored to engage a flight of four MiG-17s near Hanoi. Each crew shot down a MiG-17 with Sparrows. On 10 July 1965, during a mission over North Vietnam, two 45th TFS

Two F-4B-26-MC Phantoms, 153011/NH-104 and 153017/NH-107 of VF-213 'Black Lions', from the USS *Kitty Hawk* in the Gulf of Tonkin on 23 January 1968. Both aircraft are carrying ten Mk 82 bombs, two Sparrow and two Sidewinder missiles and a centreline drop tank. Note the newly introduced fin-tip antennas. *(USN)*

F-4Cs piloted by Capts Kenneth E. Holcombe and Arthur C. Clark, and Capts Thomas S. Roberts and Ronald C. Anderson, shot down two MiG-17s for the first USAF air-to-air combat victories of the Vietnam War.

Colonel Robin Olds

Remarkably, from January to June 1967, USAF jets shot down 46 MiGs, including seven MiG-17s by two Phantoms and five F-105s on one day, 13 May. From April to July 1967 the USN accounted for a dozen MiGs. In May 1967 Colonel Robin Olds, Commanding Officer (CO) of the 8th TFW 'Wolfpack' at Ubon RTAFB, became the leading MiG-killer in South-East Asia, adding to his World War Two score of 13 enemy aircraft destroyed. On 2 January a force

of F-4Cs of the 8th TFW, using new electronic jamming pods and simulating an F-105 strike, successfully engaged the North Vietnamese Air Force (NVNAF) and destroyed seven MiG-21s without loss. One fell to the 'Wolfpack' CO, Colonel Robin Olds, with 1/Lt Charles C. Clifton as his back-seater. Four days later, the F-4Cs flew a similar mission profile to that flown by unarmed reconnaissance aircraft, resulting in the destruction of two more MiG-21s. On 10 March, Capt. Max C. Brestel of the 354th TFS, 355th TFW became the first USAF pilot in South-East Asia to destroy two MiGs in a single sortie. Flying with Lt Lafever as his back-seater, Olds got a second victory on 4 May when he shot down a MiG-21 near Phuc Yen. On 14 May Major James A. Hargrove, Jr and Capt.

James T. Craig, Jr, piloting F-4Cs of the 48th TFS, 366th TFW, destroyed two MiG-17s using the Vulcan gun pod.

On 20 May the 8th TFW, led by Colonel Robin Olds with his back-seater Lt Steve Croker, were escorting F-105s en route to their rail target north of Haiphong when they were involved in a battle with MiG-17s. It was the 'exact replica of the dogfights in World War Two,' Olds was to recall. 'Our flights of F-4s pulled into the MiGs like a sledge-hammer, and for about a minute and a half to two minutes it was the most confused, vicious dogfight I have ever been in. There were eight F-4Cs, 12 MiG-17s, and one odd flight of F-105s on their way out from the target, who flashed through the battle area. The first MiG I lined up was in a gentle left turn, range about 7,000 ft [2134 m]. My pilot achieved a boresight lock-on, went full system, narrow gate, interlocks in. One of the two Sparrows fired in

ripple guided true and exploded near the MiG. My pilot saw the MiG erupt in flame and go down to the left.

'We attacked again and again, trying to break up that defensive wheel. Finally, once again, fuel considerations necessitated departure. As I left the area by myself, I saw that lone MiG still circling and so I ran out about ten miles [16 km] and said that even if I ran out of fuel, he was going to know he was in a fight. I got down on the deck, about 50 ft [15 m], and headed right for him. I don't think he saw me for quite a while. But when he did, he went mad, twisting, turning, dodging, and trying to get away. I kept my speed down so I wouldn't overrun him and I stayed behind him. He headed up a narrow little valley to a low ridge of hills. I knew he was either going

An F-4J of VF-142 'Ghostriders' launches from the USS *Constellation* (CVA-64) in the Gulf of Tonkin on 24 February 1970. *(USN)*

This Sparrow- and Sidewinder-armed F-4B-27-MC, 153045/NH-211, of VF-114 'Aardvarks' from the USS *Kitty Hawk* (CVA-63), was photographed over the Gulf of Tonkin in March 1968. *(USN)*

to hit that ridge up ahead or pop over the ridge to save himself. The minute he popped over I was going to get him with a Sidewinder.

'I fired one AIM-9 which did not track and the MiG pulled up over a ridge, turned left, and gave me a dead astern shot. I obtained a good growl [an aural cue that the Sidewinder was locked onto the target]. I fired from about 25 to 50 ft [8 to 15 m] off the grass and he was clear of the ridge by another 50 to 100 ft [15 to 30 m] when the Sidewinder caught him. The missile tracked and exploded 5 to 10 ft [1.5 to 3 m] to the right side of the aft fuselage. The MiG spewed pieces and broke hard left and down from about 200 ft [61 m]. I overshot and lost sight of him.

'I was quite out of fuel and all out of missiles and pretty deep in enemy territory all by myself, so it was high time to leave. We learned quite a bit from this fight. We learned you don't pile into these fellows with eight planes all at once. You are only a detriment to yourself.'

More kills

On 10 August 1967, Lt Guy H. Freeborn and his RIO Lt Bob Elliott, and Lt-Cdr Robert C. Davis and his RIO Lt-Cdr Gayle O. 'Swede' Elie, of VF-142 aboard *Constellation*, shot down two MiG-21s. On 17 December 1967, Capt. Doyle Baker, USMC, and his RIO 1/Lt John D. Ryan, Jr, destroyed a MiG-17 while flying an F-4D of the 13th TFS, 432nd TRW. On 12 August 1972 Capt. Lawrence G. Richard, USMC, and his Navy back-seater, Lt-Cdr Michael Ettel, downed a MiG-21 while flying an F-4E of the 58th TFS, 432nd TRW. The only all-Marine kill of the war occurred on 11 September 1972 when an F-4J flown by Maj. Lee T. Lasseter and his RIO, Capt. John D. Cummings, of VMFA-333 from the USS *America*, shot down a MiG-21. SAMs subsequently brought down the F-4J crew and their wing position aircraft, but all four Marine aviators were rescued and returned to their carrier.

The period 10 May to 15 October 1972 is memorable in that it produced all four American aces (three USAF and one US Navy) of the Vietnam War. Air-to-air victories were down to team effort, none more so than the five scored by Capt. Richard S. 'Steve' Ritchie of the 555th TFS, 432nd TFW (the only USAF fighter pilot ace of the war in South-East Asia). On 10 May, Ritchie and his WSO, Capt. Charles 'Chuck' B. DeBellevue, shot down a MiG-21, destroying two more on 8 July, and one on 28 August. Ritchie's fifth kill, a MiG-21, which went down on 31 May, was achieved with Capt. Lawrence H. Pettit as his back-seater. Ritchie relied on his back-seater and the support and mutual assistance of his flight and, moreover, it would have been impossible for Ritchie to score his victories without 'Red Crown' and 'Disco', the two supporting radars that pinpointed MiGs and friendly aircraft in Vietnam. The two other USAF aces achieved their ace status while flying as back-seaters. Capt. Chuck DeBellevue, who flew with Ritchie on 10 May, himself destroyed six aircraft (four MiG-21s and two MiG-19 'Farmers') during the period 10 May to 9 September 1972, and Capt. Jeffrey S. Feinstein, of the 13th TFS, flew with four pilots to get five MiG-21s between 16 April and 13 October 1972.

Cunningham and Driscoll

On 10 May 1972, Lt Randall 'Randy' H. Cunningham (pilot) and Lt (jg) William P. Driscoll (RIO) of VF-96, became the first American fliers to qualify as aces solely as a result of Vietnam air action, when they downed their third, fourth and fifth MiGs before their F-4J was hit by a SAM and went down off the coast. Both men were quickly rescued from the sea and returned to the *Constellation* where the two fliers, who had scored their two previous victories on 19 January and 8 May when they destroyed a MiG-21 and a MiG-17, respectively, related their victories to their colleagues. Cunningham and Driscoll – Callsign SHOWTIME 100 – had begun their mission as part of the flak support package for a strike group attacking Hai Duong rail yard. After delivering their ordnance, they were attacked from 7 o'clock by two MiG-17s firing cannon. SHOWTIME 100's wingman called 'break' and the MiGs overshot. The F-4J crew fired a Sidewinder which hit a MiG and it burst into flames before impacting the ground. Eight MiG-17s were then seen in an anti-clockwise orbit around the target area at 3048–4572 m (10,000–15,000 ft) and four more dived in column from the north-east. Just south of Hai Duong, SHOWTIME 100 fired its second Sidewinder, which knocked the tail off a MiG-17 whose pilot ejected. SHOWTIME 100 met its third victim head-on. Cunningham pulled up into a vertical scissors manoeuvre with the MiG-17, which was firing its cannon. After about three minutes the

MiG pilot tried to disengage, but Cunningham manoeuvred into the enemy's 6 o'clock position and fired another Sidewinder. The MiG-17 pitched over and impacted the ground with a resulting explosion and fireball. Cunningham and Driscoll attempted to exit the target area but were jumped by a fourth MiG-17. The F-4J crew attempted to engage, but broke off when another F-4J crew called four more MiG-17s at their 6 o'clock position. Cunningham broke away and accelerated toward the Gulf of Tonkin, but at 4877 m (16,000 ft) his F-4J was hit by an SA-2 fired from the vicinity of Nam Dinh. No RHAWS alert was observed by the crew, although Cunningham spotted the SAM just before impact and Driscoll observed an orange cloud after the impact. The Phantom's hydraulic systems progressively failed and both crew were forced to eject about 5 nm (9 km; 5.6 miles) from the mouth of the Red River. Cunningham and Driscoll were rescued by a helicopter from the USS *Okinawa* and returned uninjured to the *Constellation*.

The 137th and last USAF kill of the Vietnam War, a MiG-21, was claimed on 8 January 1973 by the F-4D crew of Capt. Paul D. Howman and 1/Lt Lawrence K. Kullman of the 4th TFS, 432nd TFW. In the final count, USAF F-4 crews were credited with 107.5 MiG victories. The last occasion on which a USN F-4 shot down a MiG was on 12 January 1973, when Lt Victor T. Kovaleski and his RIO Lt James A. Wise, of VF-161, in an F-4B from the USS *Midway*, destroyed a MiG-17 with two Sidewinders over the Gulf of Tonkin. This was also the last aircraft shot down by US aircraft in the Vietnam War. (Two days later Kovaleski and his RIO, Ensign Dennis Plautz, were shot down by AAA fire while escorting a reconnaissance mission near Thanh Hoa. Both were rescued by helicopter.) Navy F-4 crews were credited with the destruction of 57 MiGs from June 1965 to January 1973.

Operation *Desert Storm*

The next conflict to involve US Phantoms was Operation *Desert Storm*, the Gulf War of 1991. It was also their swan song in battle. Though their numbers were few in a conflict viewed appropriately as the first real 'electronics war', fast-ageing F-4G Wild Weasels, crammed with avionics, performed superbly in a hunter-killer partnership with F-16s. Following the Gulf War, the 52nd TFW was assigned to Operation *Southern Watch* to patrol the no-fly zone over southern Iraq on F-4G defence suppression/destruction missions in conjunction with Wild Weasel F-16C/Ds. In 1995, the only active-duty USAF unit flying F-4G Wild Weasel sorties was the 561st FS at Nellis AFB, Nevada. Major Tom Pfeiffer, one of the pilots, had flown over 130 F-4G missions over Iraq enforcing the no-fly zone, having scored a SAM site kill during *Desert Storm*. Of firing a missile at a SAM radar he recalled: 'There was a loud rumble that sounded like a bottle rocket going off, then whoosh! It

comes off the wing. It's really exciting, and after all the training and practice, I felt a real sense of accomplishment.' His father-in-law flew F-15s and before that was a Wild Weasel pilot himself. Describing the no-fly zone missions Pfeiffer said, 'Occasionally [the Iraqi troops] turn on their early warning radar to get a quick view of where we're flying. They've gotten quieter and quieter with each temporary-duty rotation. Sometimes we'll fly 24-hour operations, and sometimes we'll have crews up for just a couple of hours or half a day. We try to keep them off balance so they can't predict when or where we'll be. We don't jam the enemy's radar, the only thing we jam are HARM missiles down the enemy's throat! Flying the F-4G is like driving a classic '68 Corvette. It's just fantastic! Sheer, raw power.'

What a superb epitaph for one of the world's truly great aircraft.

4. Variants: F-4C to RF-4X

F-4C (F-110A)

When, in March 1962, the F-4C, or F-110A as it was then known, became the primary air-superiority fighter and conventional attack or nuclear strike aircraft in TAC, it was the first time a Navy aircraft had been adopted as a major combat type for the USAF. The F-4C outwardly differed little from the USN's F-4B, retaining the folding wing and arrester hook, although the Navy's probe-and-drogue air-to-air refuelling system was replaced by a receptacle on top of the fuselage for the USAF's boom-type flight refuelling system. Power was provided by two 75.60-kN (17,000 lb st) afterburning thrust J79-GE-15 engines with a built-in cartridge starting system. Dual controls were installed in the rear cockpit so that the USAF could operate the F-4 as a two-pilot (Aircraft Commander (AC) and Pilot) aircraft. Later the rear crew member was normally called the WSO or more familiarly,

Above: F-4C Phantoms (F-4C-18-MC 63-7524 nearest, F-4C-17-MC 63-7446, top) air-to-air refuelling with a Boeing KC-135A Stratotanker in January 1976. *(McDonnell Douglas)*

Opposite: F-4C-22-MC 64-0713, equipped with Sparrow III AAMs, bombs and wing tanks. *(USAF)*

'Wizzo'. The wheels were bigger than those on the navy aircraft, with low-pressure tyres and anti-skid braking systems, requiring deeper wells with a slight bulge above and below the inner wing panels. In keeping with its dual mission, the F-4C carried a wide array of electronic equipment. This included an A/A-24G Central Air Data Computer (CADC); AN/ASQ-19 communications/navigation/identification (CNI) pack; AN/ASA-32 Automatic Flight Control Sub-system (AFCS); a Litton AN/ASN-48 (LN-12A/B) inertial navigation system (INS); AN/ASN-46 navigation computer and AN/APN-155 altimeter. The AN/APQ-100 fire control system (FCS), radar and optical sight had a new rear cockpit scope, which produced an improved mapping display. Additionally, AN/APA-157 radar set group equipment; the AN/ARW-77 air-to-ground missile (AGM) control system for the

F-4C-20-MC 63-7615, of the 52nd TFW, 17th Air Force at Spangdahlem AB, West Germany. *(USAFE)*

AGM-12 Bullpup; AN/AJB-7 all-altitude bombing system, TD-709/AJB-7 sequential timer and AN/APR-25/-26 RHAWS were installed.

Missile armament options consisted of four AIM-7 Sparrow IIIs in recesses beneath the fuselage, AIM-4 Falcon or AIM-9 Sidewinders underwing, and AGM-12 Bullpup, AGM-45 Shrike and AGM-65 Maverick AGMs. The General Electric M61A-1 Vulcan 20-mm cannon could be carried in a pod under the wing or on the centreline. In the SUU-16/A pod the gun was mechanically driven by means of a ram air turbine (RAT), while in the SUU-23/A it was powered by an internal electric motor driven by gun gas. The gun could fire 1,200 rounds of ammunition. Other external stores included retarded and unretarded bombs (conventional, cluster, fire, chemical, leaflet, practice, or nuclear – with laser- or electro-optically-guided weapons coming later), and rocket launchers. The F-4C could also carry one 600-US gal (2271 litre) tank on the centreline rack and/or one 370-US gal (1400 litre) tank beneath each wing to

supplement the internal tankage of 7465 litres (1,972 US gal) in six fuselage bladder tanks and two integral wing tanks. The maximum stores load was 7258 kg (16,000 lb).

The first F-4C (62-12199 – the 310th Phantom built), was flown on 27 May 1963. Altogether, some 583 F-4Cs were built, with deliveries to the USAF continuing from 20 November 1963 to 4 May 1966. The type equipped 23 TAC squadrons. Thirty-six F-4Cs of the 81st TFW were given to Spain, where they were designated as C.12 aircraft, in 1972. During the Vietnam War, 36 F-4Cs were temporarily configured for the EF-4C Wild Weasel lethal SEAD role.

RF-4C

In May 1962, McDonnell began modification of two F-4Bs (as 62-12200/12201) and four YRF-110A development aircraft (63-4770/4773) as prototypes for an all-weather reconnaissance Phantom for the USAF. In 1963 testing of optical and electronic reconnaissance systems was begun at Holloman AFB and the first YRF-4C, with an extended nose but without cameras and other reconnaissance systems, first flew on 9 August 1963. On 30 September the second YRF-4C, with just high and low panoramic and frame cameras installed, made its maiden flight. Intended as a replacement for the RF-101C in the all-weather, day/night, high/low reconnaissance role, the first J79-GE-15 powered RF-4Cs entered operational service in September 1964 with the 16th TRS, becoming combat ready in August 1965. The RF-4C had a radius of action approaching 1609 km (1,000 miles). Although it was unarmed, the RF-4C was capable of carrying a nuclear store on its centreline. The new nose, 83.8 cm (33 in) longer than the standard F-4C nose and more tapered, housed a small AN/APQ-99 or -162 forward-looking radar with mapping, terrain-following and terrain collision avoidance modes. In the camera bay immediately behind were forward oblique, lateral and panoramic cameras, which could be configured for low-altitude day, low-altitude night or high-altitude day missions. In the standard basic

configuration a 6-in (152-mm) KS-87 camera providing forward/oblique/vertical cover for low-level day or night missions was carried (in the forward location); a 3-in (76.2-mm) KA-56 camera provided vertical panoramic cover for low-level daylight missions (centre) and at the rear a 12-in (304.8-mm) KA-55 camera in a stabilised mounting provided vertical panoramic cover for high-level daylight missions.

Located in the underside of the nose was a large AN/APQ-102 INS, and a SLAR which gave high-definition film radar pictures along each side of the aircraft's flightpath. Behind was an AN/AAS-18A IR linescan system, which produced a clear, thermal-image film picture by day or night of the same area. The Electronic Speciality ALR-17 ELRAC (Electronic Reconnaissance Camera) used in conjunction with the cameras produced automatic identification and classification of hostile radars on photo maps.

An AIL ALQ-6 I Elint (electronic intelligence) airborne receiver and recording system could be carried on the centreline pylon in place of a fuel tank. An Itek APR-25 crystal video receiver was normally fitted to produce a course bearing of hostile threats and this was usually associated with the AN/APR-26 missile-launch-warning receiver. Other devices were the ALQ-101 combined noise and repeater jammer and the ASN-56 inertial system. A large 'photo cart' array in the rear fuselage, could, upon command, eject flash cartridges vertically upwards for night photography. A powerful ARC-105 high-frequency (HF), single-side band (SSB) radio for instant contact with ground bases at the limits of range (with line-of-sight limitation), where ultra-high frequency (UHF) would be totally ineffective, was the first of its type fitted to a supersonic aircraft and the entire fin leading edge served as the shunt aerial. In most configurations some cameras, such as the low panoramic installations, could process their film in flight and eject the developed cassette in a protective capsule over a ground command post before returning to base.

Other standard equipment included AN/ASQ-88B CNI; RO-254/ASQ sound recorder; AN/ASN-46A navigation computer; AN/ASA-32J AFCS; AN/AAS-18A IR detecting set; AN/ASN-55 altitude-heading reference equipment; AN/ASN-56 INS; AN/APQ-102 radar-mapping set; AN/APQ-99 radar set; AN/APN-159 radar altimeter; AN/ASQ-90 data display set; KS-74A data recording camera set; LS-58A aircraft camera mount set; LA-311A aircraft camera parameter control; LA-285A photoflash camera control detector; AN/ALR-17 countermeasures receiving set; AN/APR-25 homing and warning subsystem; AN/APR-26 warning set; AN/ALQ-71/-72 and -87 ECM pods, and MX-7933/A interference blanker. A few RF-4Cs were given AN/ARN-92 LORAN-D

(Long-Range Navigation-D) equipment with a distinctive 'towel rail' antenna atop the fuselage. ECM upgrades, notably RHAWS and other sensors, were added throughout the RF-4C's service life. By 1986, 24 RF-4Cs had been fitted with the Litton Amecom AN/ALQ-125 TEREC (Tactical Electronic Reconnaissance sensor, with data-link equipment for transmission in near real-time), enabling passive precision location of ground-based enemy radar and communications systems in a fully automatic mode. Enemy transmissions could be analysed by computer, correlated with a detailed transmitter bank and processed into a hostile electronic order of battle (HEOB) display in the rear cockpit. TEREC was intended to operate in an intense EW environment with the F-4G Advanced Wild

RF-4C-31-MC 66-0449, of the 10th Tactical Reconnaissance Wing, is shown here in formation with an F-5E Tiger II of the 527th Tactical Aggressor Squadron. The 527th TAS was assigned to the 10th TRW to help train the Wing's crews in air-to-air combat. The 10th TRW received its first RF-4C on 12 May 1965. On 30 June 1987, the 1st TRS, 10th TRW completed transfer of its 20 RF-4Cs to TAC's 26th TRW at Zweibrücken AB, West Germany. The 26th TRW was deactivated there on 31 July 1991, ending the reconnaissance portion of the USAFE's mission. *(USAFE)*

Weasel (in trail) and the EF-111A Raven to achieve optimum results. Other improvements were the AN/ARN-101 navigational unit, the Electronic Wide-Angle Camera System (EWACS), the Ford AN/AVQ-26 Pave Tack forward-looking IR (FLIR)/laser designator system with limited all-weather capability, and an upgraded forward-looking radar.

A total of 498 production RF-4Cs were delivered to the USAF in the period June 1964 to December 1973 (four more were diverted to Spain as CR.12 machines), equipping twelve TAC and three ANG squadrons. In 1970–71, an RF-4C fitted with a HIAC-1 LOROP camera mounted in a large ventral pod, was used as part of Project *Peace Jack* to provide the Israeli Defence Force/Air Force (IDF/AF) with the capability of photographing deep into Arab countries from around 15240 m (50,000 ft) without intruding into their airspace. USAF RF-4Cs fitted with the HIAC-1 pod flew similar flights along the North Korean and Eastern European borders. In 1989, 12 ex-USAF RF-4Cs were acquired by South Korea.

DF-4B

This designation was used for a handful of F-4Bs modified by the USN as drone director aircraft.

EF-4B

A few F-4Bs were modified as EF-4B aircraft for use by VAQ-33 in the electronic aggressor role. They carried countermeasures pods and jammers beneath their wings.

NF-4B

F-4Bs permanently modified as development and research aircraft were redesignated NF-4B.

QF-4B/E/G

The third F-4B (148365) was converted by the NADC at Warminster, Pennsylvania, to QF-4B drone configuration. The aircraft's weapons systems were removed and replaced with radio and telemetry equipment suitable for its new use as a supersonic manoeuvring target for missile development work. 148365 was delivered in

spring 1972 and was followed by 44 more F-4B/QF-4B conversions. They served at the Naval Missile Center (NMC, later redesignated PMTC) at NAS Point Mugu, California, and the Naval Ordnance Test Station (NOTS, later NWC) at NAS China Lake, California. In 1999 some QF-4E/Gs and QRF-4Cs were still in use with the 53rd WEG, of the 82nd ATS at Tyndall AFB, Florida, and Det 1 at Holloman AFB, New Mexico.

EF-4C Wild Weasel

In 1965 the North Vietnamese started receiving SA-2 'Guideline' SAMs from the Soviet Union and began basing them around Hanoi. Attacks on the missile sites were very costly – the first USAF aircraft to be destroyed by an SA-2 was an F-4C which was hit on 24 July 1965 – as the attacking aircraft were forced to fly low through AAA fire to pin-point the sites; new tactics had to be devised to neutralise the missile sites. The USAF response was to develop Wild Weasel defence suppression versions of the North American F-100F Super Sabre, the Republic F-105F Thunderchief and lastly, the F-4C. These aircraft were fitted with RHAWS equipment that could home in on the SA-2's radar ('Fan Song'). The anti-missile operations fell under the code-name *Iron Hand*. At first, joint F-100F/F-105D and then 'EF-105F'/F-105D 'hunter-killer' teams were used and in 1966 the AGM-45 Shrike ARM (anti-radar missile) was first used. Wild Weasel losses were high, no less than 48 'Weasels' being lost between 1965 and 1973.

By the time of the *Linebacker* campaigns in 1972, the 'killer' component of the 'Weasel' teams was composed of F-4 Phantoms, but the EF-4C project was never as successful as the 'EF-105F' or more highly developed F-105G. The EF-4C's internal space was insufficient to house the RHAW equipment and it could not give the distance to a radar site, nor could it fire the 816-kg (1,800-lb) AGM-78 Standard ARM missile, which had been introduced in 1968 to replace the Shrike on *Iron Hand* missions, although, in fact, Shrike outlasted Standard ARM in service. The EF-4C equipment also

F-4D-29-MC 66-0229 of the 81st TFW at RAF Bentwaters, Suffolk, early in 1978. On 4 October 1965 the 81st began receiving the F-4C. *(USAFE)*

suffered from electronic interference, while the panoramic receiver pod mounted in the starboard rear Sparrow recess was subject to vibration. A major redesign was carried out and beginning in mid-1969, 36 F-4Cs were modified to the Wild Weasel 4 configuration with AN/APR-25 RHAWS and AN/APR-26 SAM launch warning system. Often an AN/ALQ-119 noise and deception active ECM pod was carried under the forward fuselage. In 1973, EF-4Cs were retrofitted with an AN/ALR-46 ECM and an AN/ALR-53 long-range homing receiver. Half the EF-4C aircraft were stationed in Europe and the other half operated with the 67th TFS at Kadena on Okinawa. In October 1972 this unit moved to Korat, Thailand, where it flew 460 sorties over North Vietnam in support of *Linebacker I* and *Linebacker II* without loss.

F-4D

The F-4C had essentially been a Navy design adapted for USAF use, and when, in March 1964, the USAF received funding to proceed with an improved Phantom version, it determined that from the outset the new model would be developed with its requirements in mind. Experience with the F-4C in Vietnam showed that what was needed was improved avionics to

increase air-to-air gunnery capability and air-to-ground weapon delivery accuracy. An AN/ASQ-91 weapon release computer enabling the new version to deliver 'smart' bombs or precision guided munitions (PGMs) was therefore installed in the No. 1 fuel tank bay, together with an AN/ASG-22 lead computing optical sight system (LCOSS) and an improved ASN-63 INS. A partly solid-state APQ-109A FCS radar set was installed in the nose to give an air-to-ground ranging capability. To supply the increased demand for electrical power, the alternators were uprated to 30 kVA. Proposals to fit a terrain following radar (TFR) system, a nose-mounted gun and Pratt & Whitney TF30 turbofans were rejected as too expensive and would have reduced commonality between USN and USAF F-4 models. Most F-4Ds were fitted with the AN/APA-165 radar set group and some received the AN/APA-157 radar set group, similar to that installed in all F-4Cs. Other equipment fitted as standard included A/A-24G CADC; AN/ASQ-l5 CNI; AN/ASA-32 AFCS; AN/ASN-46A navigation computer; AN/APN-l55 altimeter; AN/ASG-22 computing sight; AN/ARW-77 AGM-12 control system; AN/AJB-7 all-altitude bombing system; TD-709/AJB-7 sequential timer; and AN/APS-107A RHAWS.

The F-4D was first flown on 7 December 1965 and service deliveries began in March 1966, with the first examples reaching combat units in

Vietnam in 1967. Eventually, all F-4Cs in Vietnam were replaced by the F-4D. During its development the F-4D was designed with replacement of the AIM-9 Sidewinder in mind, but the war in South-East Asia revealed that its intended successor, the IR AIM-4D Falcon, offered little improvement. In combat, pilots discovered to their dismay that the Falcon needed much more pre-launch preparation than

the Sidewinder and only a direct hit would destroy an enemy aircraft because, unlike the existing missile, Falcon lacked a proximity fuse. Eventually, the Phantom's inboard pylons were returned to their previous specifications for four Sidewinders (the F-4D retained the four SARH Sparrows carried by previous models in semi-submerged wells under the fuselage). In service, the electronic suit of the F-4D was frequently

F-4B 62-12200, which became the original F-4C prototype, was also used as the aerodynamic prototype for the RF-4C and F-4E. In 1971 it was used to test the leading-edge manoeuvring slats fitted to late production F-4Es, before being fitted with a slotted stabilator and flown with a beryllium rudder and other composite components. 62-12200 was then modified as a test-bed for a fly-by-wire control system, flying in this configuration for the first time on 29 April 1972. Lastly, it was rebuilt as the F-4CCV (control-configured vehicle) with full-power canard surfaces, direct-lift trailing edges and fly-by-wire as part of the Precision Aircraft Control Technology (PACT) programme, flying in this configuration for the first time on 29 April 1974. In January 1979, 62-12200 was presented to the Air Force Museum at Wright-Patterson AFB, Ohio. *(McDonnell Douglas)*

F-4B (F-4E) 62-12200 on an early test flight on 11 February 1972, showing the slatted wing, slatted stabilator and raised gun fairing to excellent advantage. *(McDonnell Douglas)*

upgraded to meet special operational requirements. The aircraft could carry a multiple ejector rack (MER) for bombs in lieu of the centreline drop tank and the inboard pylons could mount triple ejector racks (TERs). Some F-4Ds carried special sensors for *Igloo White* operations against the Ho Chi Minh Trail. Others carried the AN/ASQ-I53(V)-2 Pave Spike laser designator pod for LGBs in place of one of the Sparrows in one of the forward fuselage wells. Further options, which could be carried on an inboard pylon in place of Sidewinders, were the AN/AVG-10 Pave Knife laser designator pod, the Westinghouse ALQ-101 noise and deception jamming pod, the General Electric ALQ-87 barrage noise jammer pod, or other ECM equipment. AN/ARN-92 LORAN-D equipment was fitted to F-4Ds equipped with the Pave

(Precision Avionics Vectoring Equipment) systems. In 1968–69, the *Combat Tree* modification programme permitted the carriage of a full missile load and ECM equipment. The programme also made it possible for an ECM pod to be carried on the inboard pylon, which by then could mount the two AIM-9J Sidewinders on each side. Seventy-one late production F-4Ds had AN/ARN-92 LORAN navigation equipment and dorsal 'towel rails' fitted.

By the time F-4D production ceased in December 1969, some 825 aircraft had been built, comprising 793 F-4Ds for the USAF and 32 F-4Ds for the Imperial Iranian Air Force (IIAF). Beginning in August 1969, at least 36 F-4Ds were transferred by the USAF to South Korea and as many were transferred to Greece after being phased out of service by the ANG in 1989–91.

EF-4D

The EF-4D designation was applied to at least four F-4Ds modified to serve as prototypes for advanced Wild Weasel defence suppression aircraft. Two of these development aircraft (65-0657 and 65-0660) were fitted with AN/APS-107 RHAWS and a target acquisition system for AGM-78 Standard ARM missiles. Two more (66-7635 and 66-7647) served as test-beds for the AN/APS-38 warning and attack system developed by McDonnell Douglas and later adopted for the F-4G.

F-4E

As the most important version of the Phantom, the F-4E was in production from July 1967 to 1981, a total of 1,379 airframes being produced. It was built for more air forces and in larger numbers than any other variant. Its most notable feature was its internal gun, which resulted from design studies late in 1964 to meet USAF TSF (Tactical Strike Fighter) requirements, and from experience gained in the Vietnam War. The six-barrel General Electric M61A1 Vulcan 20-mm rotary cannon was installed beneath the nose with provision for 640 rounds of ammunition. (An early retrofit consisting of a longer blast diffuser and derichment system, eliminated a gun gas ingestion problem which led to engine flame-outs). The semi-recessed and external stores carriage of earlier variants was retained. In place of the J79-GE-15s of the earlier versions, the F-4E was powered by two J79-GE-17 engines with an afterburning thrust of 79.60 kN (17,900 lb st). Later, engines with low smoke combustors were used. Other modifications included the use of a slotted stabilator and the removal of the automatic wing folding mechanism.

At first, the Vulcan cannon prohibited the use of a large radar and fire control system such as those in the F-4C and F-4D, so the first YRF-4C was used to test a new nose section housing an AN/APG-30 radar and a faired external pod enclosing an M61A1 cannon. Early production F-4Es were to be equipped with a solid-state Westinghouse AN/APQ-120 set with a smaller, elliptical antenna (62.2 cm by 69.9 cm/24.5 in by 27.5 in). However, the non-availability of the radar (and the unsatisfactory performance of the AN/APS-107 RHAWS, which the F-4E was to

have received), resulted in the first 30 aircraft being delivered without radar and the first 67 without RHAWS. The APQ-109/CORDS (coherent-on-receive doppler system) pulse-doppler radar was on the drawing board, however. But, if this failed to meet performance expectations, it would mean the end of Phantom production for the USAF. Meanwhile, most of the early F-4Es were retrofitted with AN/APQ-120 and AN/APR-36/37 RHAWS.

A 360-litre (95-US gal) fuel tank was installed in the rear fuselage to balance the weight of the gun and its ammunition drum (later, internal fuel capacity was reduced from 7544 to 7022 litres (1,993 to 1,855 US gal) when the fuselage bladders were replaced by self-sealing tanks starting with Block 41 aircraft (68-0495 and upwards)). The modified F-4E prototype aircraft (temporarily redesignated YF-4E) flew for the first time on 7 August 1965. Two other YF-4E development aircraft were created later by modifying F-4C 63-7445 and F-4D 65-0713, which was also used to test a boron-fibre rudder. Fortunately, CORDS got the green light on 22 July 1966 and this radar was fitted in all F-4Es from the 35th aircraft onwards. In August, promising YF-4E test results resulted in an initial batch of 96 F-4Es being ordered as part of an F-4D contract. The first of these aircraft flew on 30 June 1967 and the first combat evaluation aircraft arrived at Udorn RTAFB in 1968.

Other avionics equipment installed as standard included A/A-24G CADC; AN/ASQ-15A CNI; AN/ASA-32 AFCS; AN/ASN-63 INS; AN/ASN-46A navigation computer; AN/APN-l55 altimeter; AN/ASG-26 (modified) computing sight; AN/ARW-77 AGM-12 AGM control system; AN/AJB-7 all-altitude bombing system; TD-709/AJB-7 sequential timer and the AN/ASQ-9l (modified) weapons release system. The Northrop AN/ASX-1 Target Identification System Electro-Optical (TISEO) unit, consisting of a TV camera with a 1200-mm (47.2-in) zoom lens mounted in a canister on the port wing leading edge was fitted from aircraft 71-237 onwards. From 1971, F-4Es also received the

F-4E-55-MC 01512 (72-1512) of the *Elliniki Aeroporia* (Hellenic air force). *(McDonnell Douglas)*

ARN-101 navigation system. During production new sensors and systems such as the ASQ-23A/B Pave Spike laser designator and range finder system and the AN/AVQ-26 Pave Tack FLIR/laser target designator were added. Late in 1977, 180 F-4Es were retrofitted with the Lear Siegler AN/ARN-101(V) system to improve the accuracy of navigation and weapons delivery. Very late F-4Es were fitted with redesigned ergonomic instrument consoles.

To increase fatigue life, the wing centre-section of early production F-4Es (and additionally, most other USAF Phantoms) was reinforced with metal straps, while late production F-4Es received thicker skin panels on the production lines. In June 1969, leading-edge slats to improve manoeuvrability were first tested, but prolonged development work delayed their incorporation during production until 1972 (beginning with 71-0238). Using modification kits produced by McDonnell Douglas, the USAF subsequently retrofitted leading-edge slats to 304 early F-4Es, and the *Nirou Havai Shahanshahiye Iran* (IIAF)

This F-4E belonged to the IDF/AF. On 1 July 1968, the *Peace Echo* agreement resulted in the delivery of 44 F-4Es (and six RF-4Es) to Israel. On 10 March 1969, a licensing and technical assistance agreement was concluded between McDonnell Douglas and Israel Aircraft Industries, allowing delivery of 240 F-4Es to the Israeli air force. *(Israel Aircraft Industries)*

similarly upgraded some of its 208 F-4Es. No fewer than 428 F-4Es were built for air forces overseas. Chief among these were 86 aircraft for the *Tsvah Haganah le Israel-Heyl ha' Avir* (IDF/AF), which were funded by the USA under FMS (Foreign Military Sales) contracts. Twelve F-4Es were acquired by the Federal German Government for use in a joint US/*Luftwaffe* training programme at George AFB, California.

When development of the high-performance RF-4X was abandoned, General Dynamics modified three IDF/AF F-4Es to a special F-4E(S) reconnaissance configuration by replacing the F-4E's radar and gun installation with a new nose housing a 66-in (167.6-cm) focal length HIAC-1 LOROP camera. The modified aircraft were redelivered to the IDF/AF in 1976–77. An indigenous Israeli Phantom development came to fruition on 24 April 1987, when an Israeli F-4E was flown powered by two Pratt & Whitney PW1120 engines.

During the build up to *Desert Storm*, six F-4Es of the 3rd TFS, 3rd TFW at Clark AFB in the Philippines deployed to Incirlik AB, Turkey. It is most likely that they were called into theatre because of their PGM capability, which included both the 2,000-lb (907-kg) GBU-15(V)-1B TV/EO modular guided bomb and the AVQ-26 Pave Tack pod. However, it seems that none took part in combat missions.

Some 116 F-4Es were converted to F-4G Advanced Wild Weasel standard.

F-4EJ and F-4EJ KAI

After an order for the *Nihon Koku Jieitai* (Japan Air Self-Defence Force or JASDF) on 1 November 1968, two F-4EJs (Japanese serials 17-8301 and 17-8302) were built in St Louis and tested by McDonnell from 14 January 1971. McDonnell delivered 11 subsequent aircraft (27-8303/8306, 37-8307/8310, and 47-8311/8313) as knock-down kits for assembly in Nagoya, Japan, by Mitsubishi Jukogyo KK (Mitsubishi Heavy Industries Ltd), which then built 127 F-4EJs under licence. The F-4EJ differed from the F-4E in being optimised for the air defence role, and was not fitted with the AN/AJB-7 bombing

F-4E-67-MC 78-0744 (for Korea), the 5,057th and last McDonnell Douglas-built Phantom, was delivered on 25 October 1979. *(McDonnell Douglas)*

17-8301, one of two St Louis-built F-4EJ pattern aircraft for the JASDF, was photographed in the USA in January 1971 before delivery to Japan in July of that year. (McDonnell Douglas)

system. Since the USAF's RHAWS was not available to the Japanese, an indigenous J/APR-2 RHAWS was installed, as was a data-link system for the Japanese BADGE (Base Air Defence Ground Environment) system. Initially, it was planned to arm the F-4EJ with Mitsubishi AAM-2 AAMs but this did not take place, and neither were leading-edge slats fitted. The F-4EJ did not initially have an in-flight refuelling receptacle, but this was added later. The F-4EJ's AN/APQ-120 radar was later replaced with an AN/APG-66J, and modified aircraft were re-designated F-4EJ KAI. They also received the Litton inertial navigation system, a HUD (head-up display), and updated RHAWS. Serial 07-8431, the first of 96 aircraft brought up to the F-4EJ KAI standard, flew on 12 December 1984. The upgraded aircraft were cleared to carry AIM-7F Sparrow and AIM-9L Sidewinder AAMs, as well as Mitsubishi ASM-1 anti-ship missiles (AShMs). The last Japanese-built F-4EJ, which was also the very last Phantom built, was delivered on 20 May 1981.

RF-4E/RF-4EJ

The RF-4E was an export version of the Phantom ordered by West Germany (88), Greece (8), Iran (16), Israel (12), Japan (14 RF-4EJs) and Turkey (8). It combined the photo and multi-sensor reconnaissance system, and modified nose of the RF-4C with much of the airframe of the F-4E, and was powered by J79-GE-17 engines. The first customer for the RF-4E was the *Luftwaffe*, which ordered 88 examples in 1968. The last of the 132 RF-4Es built by McDonnell Douglas were delivered in 1981. Under the *Peace Trout* programme *Luftwaffe* RF-4Es were fitted by E-Systems with an Elint system in place of their nose-mounted cameras. By 1982, all other German RF-4Es were equipped by Messerschmitt-Bölkow-Blohm (MBB) with a weapons delivery system to endow them with a secondary attack capability.

The RF-4EJs (47-6901/6905 and 57-6906/6914) were delivered to the JASDF from November 1974 to June 1975 and became RF-4EJ KAI machines when they were modified as reconnaissance platforms fitted with Thomson-CSF Raphael SLAR.

F-4E(F) and F-4F

In the late 1960s, the Federal German Republic needed a new air-superiority fighter to replace its existing force of Lockheed F-104G Starfighters. Among the American aircraft on offer was a single-seat fighter version of the Phantom, the F-4E(F), which, together with the Lockheed CL-1200 Lancer (a next generation version of the F-104), and the Vought V-1000, was a contender in a 1969–71 US competition for a low-cost export fighter or 'international fighter' (IFX). The competition was won by the Northrop F-5E Tiger II, but the *Luftwaffe* still favoured the F-4E(F) although, in the event, the two-seat Phantom configuration was chosen when orders for 175 examples were placed. The German two-seater was designated F-4F and first flew on May 1973, with deliveries taking place from June 1973 to April 1976 (German serials 3701/3875 which, for contract management purposes, also received USAF serials 72-1111/ 1285). Twelve F-4Fs (unofficial designation TF-4F), which were used to train *Luftwaffe* crews at George AFB in California, were subsequently flown to Germany and restored to the operational F-4F configuration. MBB and VFW-Fokker produced major F-4F assemblies in West Germany, and Motoren-und-Turbinen-Union Munchen GmbH built the aircraft's J79-MTU-17A engines under licence from General Electric. A Goodyear SLAR and a real-time data link for ground processing of reconnaissance information were included.

The F-4F differed from late production F-4Es in not having an in-flight refuelling receptacle, or a No. 7 fuel tank and no provision was made for surface-attack systems and TISEO. An unslotted tailplane replaced the slotted stabilator, while the F-4F was designed to use the leading edge manoeuvring flaps developed by McDonnell Douglas for the A-4 in Project *Agile Eagle*, as first flown in 1969. The F-4F also lacked provision for carrying Maverick and Shrike AGMs, or Walleye guided bombs. it was also not equipped for Falcon or Sparrow AAMs. However, the F-4Fs were later retrofitted with in-flight refuelling receptacles and armed with Sparrow AAMs under the *Peace Rhine* programme. In the early 1990s, under the ICE (Improved Combat Efficiency) programme, 75 F-4Fs of JG 71 and JG 74 were upgraded by MBB. Their AN/APQ-120 radar was replaced by a licence-built AN/APG-65 and provision was made for the carriage of AIM-120 Advanced Medium-Range Air-to-Air Missiles (AMRAAMs). A laser gyro INS, digital central air data computers and a new databus were also installed. These upgrades were followed by the installation by MBB of a new INS, air data computers and

RF-4E 35+79 of *Aufklärungsgeschwader* 52, which began receiving the RF-4E at Leck from 17 September 1971 onwards, replacing the RF-104 Starfighter. The Federal German Republic ordered some 88 RF-4Es in January 1969. *(Air & General via Frank Mason)*

F-4F 37+01 of *Jagdgeschwader* 71 'Richthofen', with slatted wings. Between June 1973 and April 1976, the *Luftwaffe* received 175 F-4Fs manufactured from major assemblies produced by MBB and VFW-Fokker in West Germany and J79 engines built under licence by Motoren-und-Turbinen-Union Munchen GmbH. Under the *Peace Rhine* programme the F-4Fs were retrofitted with in-flight refuelling receptacles and armed with Sparrow AAMs. *(Luftwaffe)*

databus in 75 F-4Fs of the JBG 35 and JBG 36 fighter-bomber wings. From August 1983, the F-4F (and F-4E and RF-4E) began to be replaced by the multi-role Panavia Tornado.

F-4G (US Navy)

The F-4G was an interim version of the sophisticated F-4J for the USN. Its development begun in 1963. Twelve early production F-4Bs were fitted with an approach power compensation system, for use in a new automatic carrier landing mode, and the RCA AN/ASW-21 two-way digital data-link communications equipment. (Both these features were standard on the F-4J.) To accommodate the new systems, the No. 1 (front) fuselage fuel cell was reduced in size and a new racking compartment was inserted between it and the rear cockpit. BuNo. 150481, the first F-4G, flew on 20 March 1963.

Eleven further aircraft were so modified and all 12 F-4Gs were delivered to VF-96 at NAS Miramar in mid-1963 for trials. Finally, in October 1965 the F-4Gs went to sea with VF-213 aboard the USS *Kitty Hawk* (CVA-63) for deployment in the Gulf of Tonkin. The deployment lasted until June 1966. One F-4G was damaged beyond repair at Cubi Point and North Vietnamese AAA shot another down. The ten remaining aircraft were later returned to F-4B standard. Six were subsequently modified as F-4N aircraft, one became a QF-4N drone, while three others were lost in accidents before conversion could take place.

F-4G Wild Weasel (USAF)

This designation was adopted by the USAF to identify 116 F-4E-42-MC5 to -45-MC aircraft, which were brought up to a new configuration for use in the Wild Weasel SEAD role. The first of these aircraft (69-7254) was modified by

F-4B-14-MC BuNo. 150487, of VX-4 Air Test and Evaluation Squadron equipped with a fin-tip antenna. The aircraft was photographed over NAS Point Mugu, California, on 14 May 1970. 150487 was one of 12 F-4Bs used by the USN for service trials under the designation F-4G and was given the temporary number '275'. *(USN)*

McDonnell Douglas and began flight trials on 6 December 1975; subsequent aircraft were modified by the USAF at the Ogden Logistics Center, Hill AFB, Utah. Leading-edge manoeuvring slats were fitted and the J79-GE-117 engines were modified to make them 'smokeless'. The M61A1 gun and ammunition drum of the F-4E were removed to make room for an undernose fairing housing forward- and side-looking antennas, and line-replaceable units (LRUs) for the McDonnell Douglas AN/APR-38 radar and missile detection and launch homing system, respectively. Rearward-facing antennas were mounted in an enlarged fairing at the top of the tail fin. Primary armament consisted of anti-radiation missiles (AGM-45 Shrike, AGM-78 Standard ARM and, later, AGM-88 HARM), TV-guided or IIR (imaging IR) AGM-65 Maverick

Close-up of the forward fuselage of F-4G (previously F-4E-42-MC) 69-0263, of the 81st TFS, 52nd TFW, in September 1991. *(Andrew Woodroof)*

AGMs, Mk 84-based EOGBs and CBUs such as Rockeye, CBU-52 and CBU-58. For self-protection, F-4Gs carried jammer pods, AN/ALE-40 chaff and flare dispensers, AIM-7F Sparrow AAMs and AIM-9L Sidewinder AAMs. F-4Gs operated with the 37th TFW at George AFB, California, the 52nd TFW at Spangdahlem AB, West Germany, and the 3rd TFW at Clark AFB, Philippines.

During Operation *Desert Storm*, F-4G Wild Weasels drawn from the 81st TFS, 52nd TFW at Spangdahlem AB and the 37th TFW at George AFB, flew more than 2,800 sorties from Sheikh Isa, Bahrain, and Incirlik AB, Turkey.

This F-4J, the 3,000th Phantom built, was awaiting delivery to the USN in September 1968. *(McDonnell Douglas)*

F-4H

This designation remained unused to avoid possible confusion with the pre-1962 F4H.

F-4J and EF-4J

The F-4J was a USN replacement for the F-4B, fitted with a Westinghouse AN/APQ-59 radar with an 81.3-cm (32-in) diameter dish and look-down capability to detect and track targets flying at low altitudes, especially near the sea. Also included were an AN/AWG-10 pulse-Doppler missile control system and a Lear-Siegler AN/AJB-7 bombing system, which provided for

F-4J-34-MC BuNo. 155580, of VF-31 'Tomcatters', seen in flight over Southern Virginia on 30 July 1968. *(USN)*

ground attack capability substantially increased over that of the F-4B. Three YF-4Js (151473, 151496, and 151497) were modified from F-4B airframes and the first YF-4J (151473) flew on 4 June 1965. The first production F-4J flew on 27 May 1966. The F-4J was also fitted with the AN/ASW-25 one-way data-link for automatic carrier landing, the miniaturised CNI (Communications/Navigation/Identification) system, an improved tactical air navigation (TACAN) system, APR-32 RHAWS. In addition, its 16° drooping ailerons and slotted stabilators shortened take-off distance and reduced approach speed. To permit a greater recovery rate aboard ship, the undercarriage was re-stressed to allow a 7.1 m (23.3 ft) per second sink rate. Because of its increased all-up weight, the F-4J was powered by two J79-GE-10B engines with an afterburning thrust of 79.60 kN (17,900 lb st) and reduced smoke emissions. Other differences from the F-4B were larger mainwheel tyres (30 x 11 in (76.2 x 27.9 cm) as used on the F-4C); improved ECM sets; 30 kVA in place of 20-kVA generators, as in the F-4D; an additional fuel cell in the rear fuselage to increase internal capacity to 7563 litres (1,998 US gal); and a fixed inboard wing leading-edge. The VTAS (Visual Target Acquisition System) helmet sight and radar ground cooling

fans (AFC-555) were fitted to Blocks 45 and 46 F-4Js, with VTAS being retrofitted to most earlier aircraft. Other items retrofitted at intervals included AN/ALQ-126 ECM with antennas on the intakes, improved ejection seats and cockpit optimisation (AFC-506). In all, 522 F-4Js were delivered to the USN and USMC between December 1966 and January 1972. A few F-4Js were modified as EF-4J aircraft for use by VAQ-33 in the 'electronic aggressor' role with countermeasures pods and jammers carried beneath their wings.

DF-4J
Designation for a handful of F-4Js modified by the USN as drone director aircraft.

F-4J(UK)
Following the Falklands War in 1982, RAF Strike Command deployed Phantom FGR.Mk 2 fighters to the islands, first as a No. 29 Sqn detachment and later as a component of No. 23 Sqn. The aircraft were based at RAF Stanley to provide local air defence. To replace these Phantoms in the UK, it was announced at the end of 1982 that a new squadron (No. 74 Sqn) would be formed with refurbished USN F-4J Phantoms. These aircraft were then in storage at the Military Aircraft Storage and Disposal Center (MASDC) at Davis-Monthan AFB. It was believed that this type had commonality with

F-4J-32-MC 153905/AE-218 and F-4J-36-MC 155854/AE-210 of VF-84 'Bedevilers' from the USS *Franklin D. Roosevelt* (CVA-42), flying over the Caribbean in August 1969. *(USN)*

the RAF K and M versions, although in reality this was largely a myth. Before their transfer to Britain, the F-4Js (designated F-4J(UK) and given serials ZE350/ZE364) were overhauled and modified by the Naval Air Rework Facility at NAS North Island, California. By the end of 1983 the first of the F-4Js was undergoing strip down and corrosion control. A number of USN systems such as the AN/ASN-54 Approach Power Compensator System, the AN/ASW-25 data-link system, and the AN/ALQ-126 countermeasures set were removed and British systems and equipment such as the Telebrief secure communications system and avionics for Sky Flash AAMs, were installed. From August 1984 onwards crews were sent to California to work on the Js before flying them back to RAF Wattisham, Suffolk, in five flights, or 'Tiger Trails', of three aircraft each between August and December from San Diego, via Wright Patterson and Goose Bay to Wattisham.

F-4K (Phantom FG.Mk 1)
In 1964, Britain's incoming Wilson Government cancelled the projected Hawker Siddeley P.1154 supersonic V/STOL fighter, which was to equip

F-4J-33-MC 155552/AG-110, of VF-102 'Diamondbacks' from the attack carrier USS *Independence* (CVA-62), in September 1970. *(USN)*

the Royal Navy (RN) as a two-seat carrierborne interceptor, and the RAF, as a single-seat strike aircraft. On 27 February 1964, the Ministry of Defence (MoD) announced that the F-4 Phantom would replace the Royal Navy's de Havilland Sea Vixens instead of the P.1154. The F-4 was seen as a low-cost replacement, with the opportunity of using many airframe and avionics components of British origin and manufacture (40 to 45 per cent of each aircraft's value) with a consequent saving of jobs which would otherwise be lost by the cancellation of the P.1154.

Designated FG.Mk 1 by the Royal Navy, the main difference between the initial F-4K UK Phantom version and the standard version was the use of the Rolls-Royce Spey engine. The RB.168-25R Spey was a specially developed supersonic version of a proved turbofan, with fully variable reheat up to Mach 2, a dry rating of 54.48 kN (12,250 lb st) and a reheat rating of 91.23 kN (20,515 lb st). The early engines were designated Spey 201, but the 202/203 version became the standard powerplant on all British Phantoms (FG.Mk 1 and FGR.Mk 2). The Rolls-Royce powerplant had to be re-stressed for supersonic flight and combat manoeuvring and the Phantom's engine bay area had to be widened and new intake ducts fitted to handle a 20 per cent increase in mass flow. The lower portion of the aft fuselage had to be re-contoured and auxiliary air intake doors were added on the

F-4J-35MC 15826/AC-200 of VF-103 'Sluggers', aboard the attack carrier USS *Saratoga*, over the Mediterranean on 20 October 1969. *(USN)*

aft section of the powerplant compartment walls to allow extra air to be ingested during taxiing. More titanium was used in the tail area to withstand the Spey's hotter exhaust efflux. Compared with the J79 aircraft, the Spey-powered Phantom was decidedly inferior in speed, range and ceiling. Other differences included the use of an Elliott autopilot, Ferranti inertial nav/attack systems and a folding nose radome. The AWG-11 FCS differed from the AWG-10 used on the F-4J principally in having a radar dish that could swing sideways to reduce the aircraft's length to 16.5 m (54 ft), permitting the F-4K to fit on the small deck lifts of British carriers. To allow more effective Phantom

F-4J-40-MC 7257/104, of VF-114 'Aardvarks' with Carrier Air Wing 11, maintains a watch on a Soviet Tu-16 'Badger' on 7 December 1975. *(USN)*

F-4J-31-MC 153848/DN-16, of VMFA-333, at MCAS Beaufort, South Carolina, in May 1970. *(James T. Brady via Frank Mason)*

FG.Mk 1 operations from the smaller British carrier decks, features developed by McDonnell Douglas for the F-4J, which was then in development, were included – larger flaps; drooping ailerons and slotted tailplanes (with reduced anhedral) to increase rotational capability after catapult launches. A new double-extendable nosewheel leg, which extended to 101.6 cm (40 in), compared with the 50.8 cm (20 in) of the standard aircraft, allowed the wind-over-deck requirement for launching to be reduced by 11 kt (20.4 km/h; 12.7 mph). The main landing gear and arresting hook were strengthened to allow the F-4K to land at weights as high as 17,237 kg (38,000 lb) with a 7.3-m (24-ft) per second sink speed.

On 30 September 1964 two Spey-engined YF-4K prototypes were ordered, to be followed in 1965 by an order for 20 production FG.Mk 1s. A further 39 aircraft were ordered soon after. The British Government had insisted on a fixed-price contract as opposed to cost-plus and so orders were restricted ultimately to just 52 aircraft (although 14 were delivered direct to the RAF to

BuNo. 153783, one of the 15 F-4J Phantoms for the RAF, is shown after its short flight from storage at MASDC Davis-Monthan, Arizona, to San Diego, California, on 30 November 1983. The aircraft was completed on 9 August 1984 and given the RAF serial ZE352. *(CSDE)*

help make good deficiencies that arose from British insistence on a fixed-price contract). The first FG.Mk 1 (YF-4K) for the Royal Navy (XT595) flew at St Louis on 27 June 1966 and the first three production FG.Mk 1s (XT858, 859 and 860) were delivered to the Royal Navy on

Right: One of the original F-4Js for the RAF was dropped into the bay while being transferred by helicopter between Davis-Monthan and North Island near San Diego; an incident viewed, incidentally, by members of the British Royal Family on board the Royal Yacht *Britannia*, which was on a west-coast tour at the time. A replacement airframe had to be found to make up the full complement of 15 F-4Js for the RAF! *(CSDE)*

Below: An 892 Sqn Phantom FG.Mk 1, with the unit's 'Omega' insignia on its fin, launches from HMS *Ark Royal* with a load of ten 1,000-lb (454-kg) bombs. *(RN)*

Phantom FG.Mk 1 XT871, of No. 892 Sqn, aboard HMS *Ark Royal* in June 1971. *(RN)*

29 April 1968, to become the service's first truly supersonic fighter. In November 1978 when the Royal Navy ceased carrier operations, 16 Phantom FG.Mk 1s were transferred to the RAF to re-equip No. 111 Sqn.

F-4L

This designation was given to a number of advanced versions proposed to the USN in 1963–64, but which did not enter production. One configuration, Model 98FOA, had the aircraft powered by Rolls-Royce RB.168-25R turbofans and armed with either six medium-range Sparrow IIIs, or two long-range Phoenix AAMs.

F-4M (Phantom FGR.Mk 2)

After the abandonment of the P.1154 and the superlative BAC TSR.2, plus the subsequent cancellation of the General Dynamics F-111K, which was intended to replace the latter, on 2 February 1965 the British Prime Minister,

Harold Wilson, announced that the F-4M (Phantom FGR.Mk 2) had been chosen to replace the RAF's Hawker Hunters and English Electric Canberra bombers. It was planned that the Phantom FGR.Mk 2 would replace the Hunter FGA.Mk 9 ground-attack and FR.Mk 10 fighter - reconnaissance aircraft in No. 38 Group Air Support Command and RAF Germany until they themselves were replaced in 1971 (an event which actually occurred in 1973–74) by the SEPECAT Jaguar. At the same time, the Phantom would also replace the English Electric Lightning F.Mk 6 in the air-defence role in Europe. Two prototype YF-4Ms and 150 production aircraft were ordered in 1965–66 (although the fixed-cost arrangement in the original contract reduced the number of Phantoms for the RAF to 118, a total bolstered by 14 aircraft earmarked for the Royal Navy but delivered direct to the RAF). The first YF-4M prototype (XT852) flew on 17 February 1967. The first production FGR.Mk 2 (XT891) flew to RNAS Yeovilton on 18 July 1968.

The Phantom FGR.Mk 2 differed from the Royal Navy's FG.Mk 1 in having the

AN/AWG-12 FCS and a Ferranti inertial navigation/attack system, while the slotted stabilators, double-extensible nose leg and the drooping ailerons were all deleted. Anti-skid brakes permitted safe operation on short and/or wet runways. Armament for interception duties consisted of four fuselage-mounted Sparrow III AAMs and four Sidewinder AAMs beneath the wings. In the reconnaissance role the FGR.Mk 2 mounted a centreline multi-sensor reconnaissance pod. Made by Hawker Siddeley, this contained an EMI IR linescan and SLAR. During the mid-1970s the RAF's Phantoms underwent a wing strengthening programme to prolong their fatigue life and were fitted with a radar warning receiver (RWR) in a fairing atop the fin.

F-4N and QF-4N

By the early 1970s many of the F-4B/Js in USN and USMC service had far exceeded their design life. The decision was therefore taken to initiate a Service Life Extension Program (SLEP) by rebuilding 178 F-4Bs under Project *Bee Line*, at the Naval Air Rework Facility (NARF) at North Island, San Diego. Newly inserted structural components and complete rewiring were designed to extend the fatigue life of the aircraft, and J79-GE-10 engines with power approach compensation and smoke abatement (often removed in service) were installed. An AN/AWG-10 missile-control system and dogfight computer; AJB-7 bombing system; AN/ASW-25 one-way data-link; Sidewinder Expanded Acquisition Mode (SEAM); VTAS; air-to-air identification friend or foe (IFF); Automatic Altitude Reporting System (AIMS); miniaturised CNI; fin-top ECM; 30-kVA alternators and a GVR-10 vertical reference were all fitted as standard. In addition, larger 30 x 11.5 in (76.2 x 29.2 cm) mainwheels, slotted stabilators and fixed inboard wing leading edges were all adopted and an additional No. 7 fuel cell was added to the rear fuselage. For the USMC an Air Combat version of the F-4N was also developed, incorporating the highly successful wing manoeuvring slats that were then being introduced on the F-4E, and a digital version of the analogue AWG-10 weapon control system used by the USN. The first F-4N flew on 4 June 1972. Forty F-4Ns were later modified as QF-4N drones by the USN.

F-4P, F-4Q and F-4R

These designations were unused.

F-4S

Some 248 further F-4Js (of 302 once planned) also underwent a SLEP at NARF North Island. Each aircraft passed through a process to give it a strengthened airframe and undercarriage; a longer fatigue life; complete rewiring and updated mission equipment such as the digital AWG-10B weapon control system and new radio. Some but not all the F-4S aircraft received TACAN and although two-position leading edge

Over the Mediterranean in April 1977, F-4N BuNo. 152970 of VF-51 'Screaming Eagles', intercepts a Soviet-built Tu-22 'Blinder' bomber and maritime attack aircraft being delivered to Libya. *(USN)*

Phantom FGR.Mk 2 XV437 of No. 54 (Fighter) Sqn, loaded with drop tanks, four rocket launchers, two Sparrow missiles, a centreline reconnaissance pod and two ECM units, and XV432/N of No. 6 (Fighter) Sqn, with drop tanks, six rocket launchers, three Sparrows and a ventral gun pod, formate at low level in 1969. (MoD)

wing manoeuvring slats were not initially fitted to the first 46 F-4Ss, beginning in September 1979 the 47th and subsequent F-4S conversions received them. The first 46 F-4S machines had the slats retrofitted at McDonnell Douglas's St Louis plant. The F-4S also received 'smokeless' J79-GE-10B engines; USAF-style formation strip lights on the fin and above the wing along the fuselage; and staggered cooling ports near the nosewheel well. The first F-4S was completed in June 1975 and the first deliveries were to the USMC, beginning with VMFA-451 at Beaufort, South Carolina.

F-4P (F-4X and RF-4X)

In the mid-1970s the USAF and General Dynamics jointly embarked on programmes aimed at producing a Phantom reconnaissance aircraft capable of operating as high as 76,000 ft (23165 m) or above the ceiling of the MiG-25 'Foxbat'. These programmes were apparently undertaken either following the decision not to export the Martin RB-57F high-altitude reconnaissance aircraft to Israel or/and when it became evident, in 1972, that the carriage of the HIAC-1 camera pod by the F-4 would result in unacceptable performance penalties. (Under the *Peace Jack* programme, F-4E 69-7576 was modified to carry the General Dynamics HIAC-I LOROP camera of 66-in (167.6-cm) focal length operating through side and bottom-mounted oblique windows, altering the nose shape and increasing fuselage length by 30.5 cm (12 in).) General Dynamics proposed a very high-performance derivative of the Phantom with a long-range camera mounted in a modified nose and engine thrust markedly boosted at high altitude through the use of PCC (pre-compressor cooling). With this water-injection system boosting its speed, the aircraft was expected to have a top speed of Mach 3.2 and to cruise for 10 minutes at Mach 2.7 at an altitude of 78,000 ft (23774 m). In 1976 the Israeli Air Force provided 69-7576 for modification as an RF-4X mock-up at Edwards AFB, California. The mock-up was completed in December 1974 with external dorsal tanks for the PCC system (which fattened the fuselage shape), enlarged intakes, revised variable intake ramps, and nose-mounted HIAC-1 camera. An Israeli-developed Elta EL/M-2021 jamming system may also have been among its equipment. Various other designations, including RF-(X), RF-4E(S) and F-4X have been quoted unofficially either for the 69-7576 test-bed or for proposed developments. Without a USAF requirement for the RF-4X or its proposed F-4X fighter variant, however, development costs were soon found to be too high to justify manufacture of a few aircraft for the IDF/AF. The project never reached prototype stage and 69-7576 was modified to F-4E(S) configuration.

5. International Operators

Great Britain

Including prototypes, 170 Phantoms were delivered to Great Britain in 1968–69. These totalled four prototypes (two each for the Royal Navy and RAF), 50 Phantom FG.Mk 1s for the Royal Navy (14 of which were re-allocated to the RAF) and 116 Phantom FGR.Mk 2s (against 150 ordered). In addition, late in 1982, the MoD announced that a new squadron, No. 74 Sqn, RAF would be formed using 15 ex-USN F-4J Phantoms and these began arriving in August 1984.

The first and second YF-4Ks for the Royal Navy had flown during 1966 and they were used for trials at Edwards AFB, California, and the USN test centre at Patuxent River, where British pilots took part in the flight-test programme. In England one of the YF-4Ks was sent to Hawker Siddeley, the prime British contractor, at Holme-on-Spalding Moor, and the other went to Rolls-Royce at Hucknall. The Fleet Air Arm's (FAA's) No. 700P trials squadron was commissioned on 30 April 1968 at RNAS Yeovilton (HMS *Heron*), to receive the Phantoms for the Royal Navy. They

A Phantom FG.Mk 1 of No. 43 Sqn, based at RAF Leuchars, Fife, Scotland, escorts a Soviet Tu-95RTs 'Bear-D' reconnaissance aircraft. *(RAF Leuchars)*

A Phantom FG.Mk 1 of No. 43 Sqn and two F-4Es of the 525th TFS, 36th TFW, photographed over West Germany in 1969. (MoD)

were to replace the Sea Vixen as an all-weather, long-range, carrierborne fighter for fleet defence.

The first three Phantom FG.Mk 1s were flown direct to Yeovilton on 25 April under the code name Project *Translant* and three more followed over the next two months. The last delivery of FG.Mk 1s to Britain occurred on 21 November 1969. Training was then taken over by No. 767 Sqn, which acted as a conversion-training unit when it was formed in January 1969. It was also envisaged as being a shore-based back-up unit for those units embarked at sea (when No. 767 Sqn disbanded in August 1972, the Phantom Training Flight at RAF Leuchars trained aircrew flying the FG.Mk 1) but in the event, the only other FAA Phantom unit was No. 892 Sqn. This

squadron, which was commissioned on 31 March 1969, became carrier-qualified aboard the USS *Saratoga* (CVA-60) late in 1969. By 1970 the FAA had been reduced to two fleet carriers, HMS *Eagle* and HMS *Ark Royal*. In June that year, No. 892 Sqn was embarked aboard the *Ark Royal*, a ship destined to be the last Royal Navy carrier capable of embarking conventional fixed-wing aircraft for at least four decades. On 27 November 1978, No. 892 Sqn was decommissioned as HMS *Ark Royal* was paid off, ultimately to be replaced by anti-submarine carriers equipped with the BAe Sea Harrier in the fleet protection role. The last sixteen FG.Mk 1s in Royal Navy service were transferred to the RAF at the end of 1978.

The first production Phantom FGR.Mk 2 (XT891) flew to Yeovilton on 18 July 1968 and the first FGR.Mk 2s for the RAF were issued to No. 228 OCU (Operational Conversion Unit) at

RAF Coningsby, Lincolnshire on 23 August 1968. By 29 October 1968 the RAF order for the FGR.Mk 2 was complete. No. 6 Sqn became the first unit in the RAF to operate the Phantom, after forming at Coningsby on 7 May 1969. On 1 September No. 43 Sqn 'Fighting Cocks' reformed at RAF Leuchars (with the FG.Mk 1 diverted from the Royal Navy order) for operations over the northern part of the UK Air Defence Region. That same day, No. 54 Sqn reformed at Coningsby with the FGR.Mk 2 for the ground-attack role. In July 1970, No. 64 Sqn was allocated as No. 228 OCU's 'shadow' designation. (In 1978 the OCU assumed the responsibility of training crews for both the Phantom FGR.Mk 2 and FG.Mk 1 versions, remaining at Coningsby until 22 April 1987 when it relocated to RAF Leuchars. It was disbanded on 31 January 1991, to be replaced by the Phantom Training Flight at Wattisham under the control of No. 74 Sqn.)

Meanwhile, on 30 June 1970, No. 14 Sqn formed at Brüggen, West Germany, and was soon joined by No. 17 Sqn. On 14 December, No. 2 Sqn, a tactical-reconnaissance unit, formed at Laarbruch, its FGR.Mk 2s being fitted with the Hawker Siddeley reconnaissance pod. No. 2 Sqn was declared operational with the Phantom on 1 April 1971. On 20 July 1971, No. 31 Sqn became the last in RAF Germany to equip with the Phantom FGR.Mk 2, when it converted from the Canberra PR.Mk 7.

On 1 April 1972 No. 41 Squadron reformed with the Phantom FGR.Mk 2 at RAF Coningsby for the reconnaissance and ground-attack roles. However, in 1974 the Phantom was transferred from ground attack to air defence and when, on 29 March, No. 54 re-equipped with the Jaguar GR.Mk 1, its FGR.Mk 2 Phantoms passed to No. 111 Sqn at RAF Coningsby. 'Treble One' became operational on 1 October 1974. That summer No. 6 Sqn also began conversion to the Jaguar, and in April 1975 No. 14 Sqn also began its conversion to the type, with re-equipment completed by November. No. 17 Sqn had begun re-equipping with the Jaguar in September 1975 and in June

1976 No. 2 Sqn began its conversion, with completion by 1 October. No. 23 Sqn began conversion to the Phantom FGR.Mk 2 in mid-1975 and No. 56 Sqn converted to the aircraft between March and 29 June 1976. In April 1974, No. 29 Sqn began its conversion to the FGR.Mk 2, being based at RAF Coningsby in the air defence role from 1 January 1975. In July 1976, No. 19 Sqn at Wildenrath began receiving FGR.Mk 2s, while No. 31 Sqn converted to the Jaguar GR.Mk 1. On 1 April 1977, No. 92 Sqn at Wildenrath also completed re-equipment with the Phantom FGR.Mk 2. No. 41 Sqn operated the FGR.Mk 2 until its replacement by the Jaguar, which began in August 1976, officially reforming on the new type at RAF Coltishall on 1 April 1977. Late in 1978, No. 111 Sqn began receiving sixteen former RN Phantom FG.Mk 1s, although it was March 1980 before conversion was complete.

Starting on 17 October 1982, No. 29 Sqn supplied the first Phantom detachment to be deployed to Mount Pleasant (RAF Stanley) for the air defence of the Falkland Islands. On 30 March 1983, No. 29 Sqn transferred its Phantoms to No. 23 Sqn, when it disbanded at Wattisham, reforming the same day at RAF Stanley to replace the Phantom detachment provided by No. 29 Sqn. On 19 October 1984, No. 74 Squadron reformed at Wattisham on F-4J(UK) Phantoms to fill a gap caused by the need to deploy a UK-based FGR.Mk 2 squadron to the Falklands. (Early in 1991, the F-4J(UK)s were withdrawn and were replaced on 17 January by FGR.Mk 2s released by RAF Leuchars.) In May 1987, No. 29 Sqn ceased flying Phantoms and became the RAF's first operational Panavia Tornado F.Mk 3 interceptor squadron on 1 November that year. With the reduction of the threat in the South Atlantic, on 1 November 1988 No. 23 Sqn was redesignated No. 1435 Flight, enabling the squadron to return to the UK and reform with Tornado F.Mk 3s at RAF Leeming. No. 43 Sqn continued operating the FG.Mk 1 Phantom at Leuchars, adding the FGR.Mk 2 version in May 1988, and converting to the Panavia Tornado F.Mk 3 in September

1989. Also at Leuchars, 'Treble One' Sqn began replacing its FG.Mk 1s with the Tornado F.Mk 3 on 31 January 1990. No. 92 Sqn disbanded on 5 July 1991 and No. 19 Sqn disbanded at the end of the year. During 1992, No. 56 Sqn, No. 1435 Flight and the Phantom Training Flight all disbanded, followed, on 1 January 1993 by No. 74 Squadron.

Iran

From the late 1960s to the mid-1970s, America supported the Shah of Iran in his fight against revolutionary factions in the Middle East. In 1966 the *Nirou Havai Shahanshahiye Iran* (IIAF) ordered 32 F-4Ds and these entered service with two squadrons at Tehran-Mehrabad in 1969. The F-4Ds were ferried to Tehran-Mehrabad starting on 8 September 1968 and were used to equip the 306th FS. A second delivery of 16 F-4Ds in 1969 was used to equip a second squadron at Doshen-Toppeh. During 1974–77, 177 F-4Es and 16 RF-4Es were delivered. The F-4Ds were normally armed with the M61 Vulcan gun in a centreline pod, four Sparrows and four Sidewinders. They were used unsuccessfully against high-flying Soviet-built MiG-25 'Foxbats' and were replaced in the interception role in the mid-1970s by 80 F-14A Tomcats. The latter also took over the interception duties of the F-4Es, which were switched to a primary attack role. In 1975, the F-4Ds were also deployed to the Sultanate of Oman to help in the war against Dhofari rebels. One F-4D was shot down by ground fire.

In total Iran equipped two squadrons with F-4Ds and eight with F-4Es, at Mehrabad, Tabriz and Shiraz, and one squadron with the RF-4E. The F-4Es were equipped with APR-37 passive warning receivers to detect radar emissions and SAM launches. ALQ-72 active ECM pods could be installed in the rear pair of Sparrow recesses. For the attack role Iran purchased 2,850 Maverick AGMs for its F-4Es. All the F-4Es and RF-4Es were fitted with in-flight refuelling receptacles for refuelling from 12 Boeing 707-3J9-Cs and eight ex-TWA airliner Boeing 747s.

Following the overthrow of the Shah by the Ayatollah Khomeini in 1979, 31 of the F-4Es and 16 of the undelivered RF-4Es were embargoed by the US and placed in storage at Davis-Monthan AFB. Many Iranian pilots and senior maintenance personnel followed the Shah into exile, and the newly created Islamic Republic of Iran Air Force (IRIAF) was excessively weakened. When, in September 1980, Iraqi forces invaded Iran, the IRIAF was ill prepared to meet the threat. At first the F-4Es made deep penetration raids against military and industrial targets in and around Baghdad and supported ground operations along the disputed Shaat-al-Arab waterway and in the fighting for Abadan. Later, they were used more in a defensive role to protect oil refineries and loading facilities, as well as Tehran and other major cities, against Iraqi air raids. A combination of a lack of skilled maintenance personnel, the US embargo and mounting losses (including two F-4Es which were shot down by Saudi F-15As) resulted in few F-4D/Es remaining operational. Indeed, by 1985 only about 50 of the 220 that started the war were still serviceable. Raids were few – in January 1988 IRIAF Phantoms made rocket attacks against oil tankers in the Gulf – and when the war ended in 1988 only a small handful of F-4Es and RF-4Es remained.

South Korea

In 1969 the *Han-guk Kong Goon* (RoKAF) obtained 18 ex-USAF F-4Ds under the *Peace Spectator* programme, to replace the F-86D in the 1st FW. The first six aircraft were handed over at a ceremony at Taegu AB on 29 August. In 1972 the RoKAF transferred its F-5A/Bs to the Vietnamese Air Force and, in return, received 18 more ex-USAF F-4Ds from the USA, to re-equip another squadron. Six F-4Ds were supplied later by the USAF as attrition replacements and during 1987–88, 24 further ex-USAF F-4Ds were acquired to bring the RoKAF's two F-4D squadrons back to strength and to equip a third.

During 1977–79, 37 new F-4Es were delivered under *Peace Pheasant II* and were issued to the

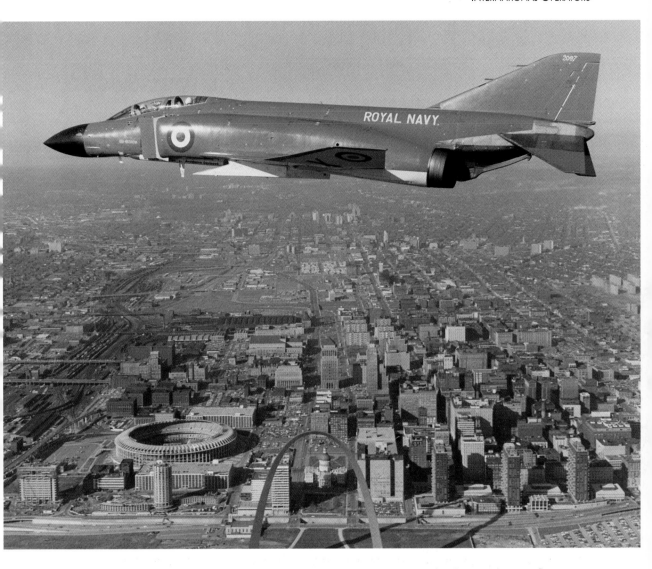

17th TFW. In 1988–89 76 ex-USAF F-4Es (and 12 ex-USAF RF-4Cs) arrived and the RoKAF had formed its fifth F-4E squadron by the end of 1989.

Israel

Following the June 1967 Six Day War, a massive re-equipment of the IDF/AF followed. On 1 July 1968 Israel and the US signed the *Peace Echo* agreement for the supply of 50 F-4Es and six RF-4Es. These entered service with three squadrons in 1969 (Israel obtained the loan of two RF-4Cs from August 1970 to March 1971,

The first YF-4K (XT595) for the Royal Navy, flying over the St Louis arch. *(McDonnell Douglas)*

pending delivery of the RF-4E order, which was increased to 12 with the delivery of a second batch). On 10 March 1969, McDonnell Douglas and Israel Aircraft Industries (IAI) concluded a licensing and technical assistance agreement and deliveries began in September 1969. In total the IDF/AF received 240 F-4Es, including 86 ordered under FMS contracts and aircraft transferred from the USAF inventory.

65

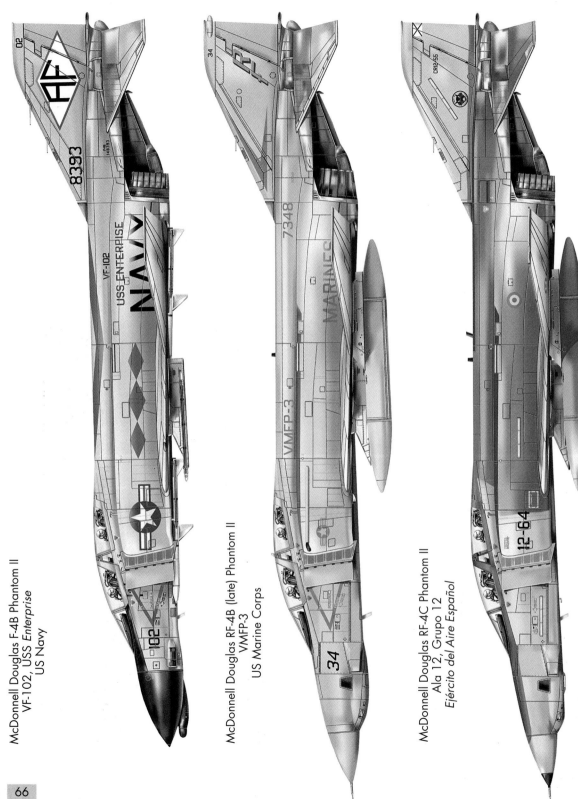

McDonnell Douglas F-4B Phantom II
VF-102, USS *Enterprise*
US Navy

McDonnell Douglas RF-4B (late) Phantom II
VMFP-3
US Marine Corps

McDonnell Douglas RF-4C Phantom II
Ala 12, Grupo 12
Ejército del Aire Español

McDonnell Douglas F-4J Phantom II
VF-96
US Navy

McDonnell Douglas F-4C Phantom II
171st FIS, 191st FIG
Michigan ANG

Above: A *Luftwaffe* RF-4E (35+15, 97452), the first RAF YF-4M Phantom FGR.Mk 2 (XT852) and a USAF F-4E-44-MC (69-7264) of the 86th TFW at Ramstein, West Germany, formate for the camera. The USAF and RAF machines have EROS (Eliminate Range-Zero System) collision avoidance pods in their front Sparrow recesses. The RF-4C has no Sparrow recess, so it carries EROS on its centreline. *(McDonnell Douglas)*

Below: Phantom FGR.Mk 2 XV424 of the RAF, was painted to celebrate the first non-stop transatlantic flight by Sqn Ldr A. J. N. Alcock, MBE and Flt Lt W. N. Brown in 1919 (although the latter's name is misspelt 'Browne' on the canopy sill) and the 30th anniversary of NATO. *(Rolls-Royce)*

Following increased tension in the region, on 22 October 1969, just six weeks after the Phantoms entered service, the F-4Es went into action with strikes against SAM missile sites in Egypt. The first Phantom air-to-air victory occurred on 11 November. In early January 1970 the first deep penetration bombing raids took place. While McDonnell Douglas A-4 Skyhawks attacked artillery and fortifications, the F-4s flew far into Egypt attacking camps and military installations in the Nile Valley near Cairo. A few days later a massive attack was carried out on targets in Cairo itself and on 13 January the IDF/AF raided SAM sites near Cairo International Airport. MiG-21MF 'Fishbed-J' interceptors made their appearance in the spring and many battles ensued. Finally, an American-sponsored cease-fire came into effect on 7 August 1970.

By 1973 Israel was faced by Arab air forces largely equipped with Soviet-supplied aircraft and hundreds of SA-2 'Guideline', SA-3 'Goa', and SA-6 'Gainful' radar-guided SAMs, as well as SA-7 'Grail' IR-directed, shoulder-launched SAMs and ZSU-23-4 Shilka radar-directed mobile AAA guns. The interlocking Arab air defence system was superior even to the AA belt protecting Hanoi during the Vietnam War. The IDF/AF had 432 aircraft in its inventory, of which Phantoms were the second most numerous aircraft, against 600 aircraft operated by Egypt and 210 by Syria. Anticipating that Israel might not be prepared for war, Egypt and Syria invaded the country on 6 October 1973 – Yom Kippur, the Jewish fast day. Initially, Israel was pegged back and the IDF/AF was obliged to mount long-range strike missions against enemy ground forces in Egypt and the Suez Canal zone before tackling the SAMs. The result was disastrous, the IDF/AF losing 33 of its 140 F-4Es (mainly to SAMs). Israel admitted to total losses of 115 aircraft (US estimates were nearer 200), 60 of them in the first week of the Yom Kippur War. To evade the SA-2, the F-4E pilots found that they had to enter the engagement zone of the SA-6, and there the only effective counter action was to dive inside and below the missile before it had time to gain high altitude and speed. Then they ran headlong into the range of the SA-7 and SA-9 and the massed array of ZSU-23-4s. Israel was supplied with AGM-45A Shrike anti-radiation missiles (ARMs), but these were largely unsuccessful against the continuous wave-guidance SA-6, which the Phantoms had great difficulty in out manoeuvring once the missiles had been launched. Eventually, the IDF/AF gained the upper hand on the Sinai Front by making massed attacks using squadrons of attacking aircraft, rather than in groups of four, while ground targets were bombed accurately using US-supplied 'smart' bombs and the F-4Es were fitted with decoy flares to counter the heat-seeking SAMs. An armistice was agreed on 24 October 1973 and Operation *Nickle Grass* ensured that Israeli losses were made good with the urgent delivery of 36 F-4Es from USAFE and TAC units.

Many modifications were made to the F-4Es throughout their service life. A non-retractable refuelling probe, canted upward and outboard to place the nozzle within easy sight of the pilot,

A Phantom FGR.Mk 2 of No.92 Sqn, over the Mediterranean near the coast of Cyprus during an APC (Armament Practice Camp) in June 1976. *(MoD)*

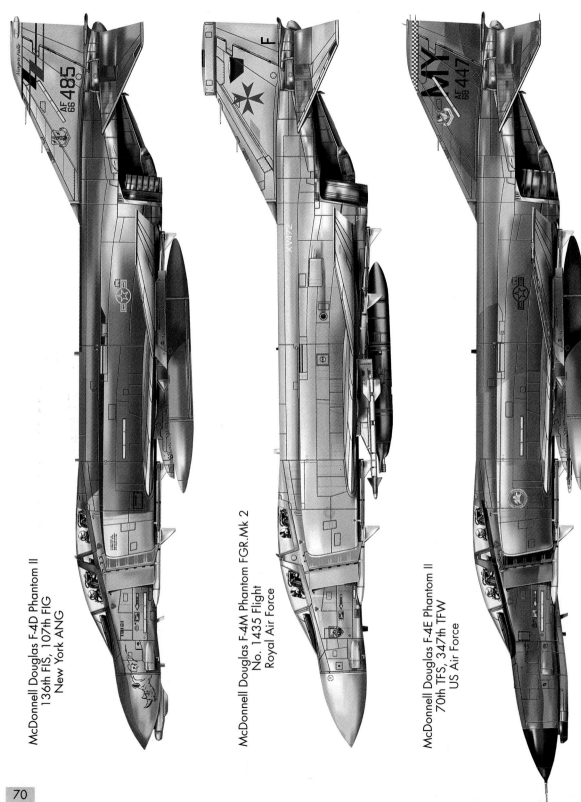

McDonnell Douglas F-4D Phantom II
136th FIS, 107th FIG
New York ANG

McDonnell Douglas F-4M Phantom FGR.Mk 2
No. 1435 Flight
Royal Air Force

McDonnell Douglas F-4E Phantom II
70th TFS, 347th TFW
US Air Force

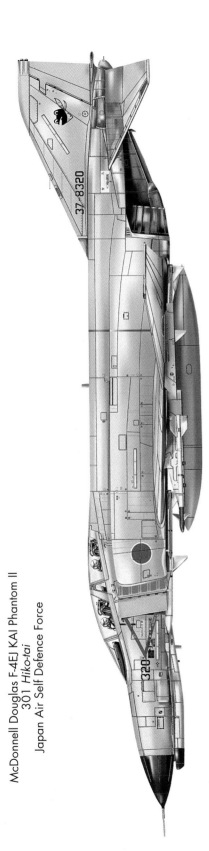

McDonnell Douglas F-4EJ KAI Phantom II
301 *Hiko-tai*
Japan Air Self Defence Force

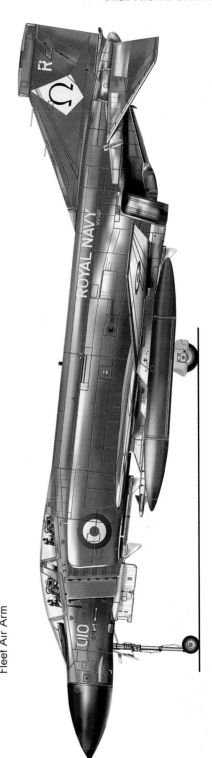

McDonnell Douglas F-4K Phantom FG.Mk 1
No. 892 Sqn
Fleet Air Arm

Phantom FG.Mk 1s XV581 of No. 43 Sqn and XT875 of No. 111 Sqn, formate with Panavia Tornado F.Mk 3 ZE812. No. 43 Sqn operated the Phantom FG.Mk 1 at Leuchars until July 1989, when its replacement by the Tornado F.Mk 3 began. Also at Leuchars, 'Treble One' Sqn began replacing its FG.Mk 1s with the Tornado in 1990. *(Tony Paxton)*

was attached to the starboard fuselage and connected to the dorsal fuel receptacle. Provision was also made for carrying indigenous Shafrir and Python AAMs, Gabriel LGBs, Elta EL/M-2021 radar, and a FLIR. A trial fitting saw the 20-mm M61A1 rotary gun replaced by two 30-mm DEFA cannon.

On 3/4 July 1976, Israeli Phantoms escorted Lockheed C-130 Hercules and Boeing 707s over the Red Sea en route to Uganda during the daring rescue of hostages in Entebbe. By 1978 some 204 F-4Es had been delivered to the IDF/AF, of which about 65 had been lost in combat and operational accidents. In June 1982 when Israeli forces invaded the Lebanon and fought against Syrian forces, F-4Es armed with ARMs and bombs attacked and destroyed Syrian SAM batteries in the Bekaa Valley. By now Israel had F-15s and F-16s and IAI Kfir C-2 fighters, which nullified the Syrian fighters. By the end of the decade, 110 F-4Es still equipped five squadrons, however. Israel planned to replace the J79 engines with 91.61-kN (20,600-lb st) thrust Pratt & Whitney PW1120 engines, fit canard surfaces, install more modern systems and equipment, and strengthen the airframes to extend service life, but budgetary considerations forced most of these improvements to be cancelled. By now most of the Phantoms were high-time aircraft and it would not be very cost-effective to modernise them.

West Germany and Germany

Towards the end of the 1960s the Federal German Republic began seeking a replacement aircraft for its Lockheed F-104G/RF-104G Starfighter force. In January 1969, 88 RF-4Es were ordered for the *Luftwaffe*, the first RF-4E flying on 15 September 1970. On 16 January 1971 this aircraft (named *Spirit of St Louis*) and three others, departed St Louis for West Germany. Further deliveries (of 42 RF-4Es each) were made to two tactical reconnaissance *Geschwader*, *Aufklärungsgeschwader* 51 (AG 51) 'Immelmann' at Bremgarten and AG 52 at Leck, where they replaced RF-l04G Starfighters. Two aircraft were delivered to *Erprobungsstelle* 61 for trials, and two others to TSLw 1 at Kaufbeuren for training.

By the 1970s changes in the MRCA-75 (Panavia Tornado) programme that deleted the single-seat version originally specified by the Luftwaffe and put back delivery of the two-seat version, opened up a gap in West Germany's fighter inventory. As a result, in 1971, the Bundestag Defence Committee ordered 175 F-4Fs as part of the *Peace Rhine* programme to replace the F-104G in two *Jagdgeschwader* (fighter wings; 30 F-4Fs each) and two *Jagdbombergeschwader* (fighter-bomber wings; 36 F-4Fs each). The first F-4F flew in May 1975 and deliveries to JG 71 'Richthofen'

at Wittmundhaffen and JG 74 'Mölders' at Neuburg began in June that year. (In German service the Phantom became known as the 'Elefunt' because of its large intakes!) Conversion training for *Luftwaffe* RF-4E and F-4F crews meanwhile, was carried out at George AFB in California, within the 35th TFW under a US/West German co-operative agreement. Fifteen of the 175 F-4Fs produced between May 1973 and April 1976 were retained for the training phase until replaced in 1977 by ten F-4Es paid for by West Germany but delivered to the USAF for use by the 20th TFS at George AFB. In 1974, JBG 36 began conversion to the F-4F at Rheine-Hopsten and by mid-1976, Nos 361 and 362 *Staffeln* were operational – during 1981, a third component, the *Zentrale Ausbilddung-seinrichtung* (ZAE, No. 363 *Staffel*) was added to the wing. The ZAE was assigned to 'Europeanisation' conversion of pilots who learned to fly the F-4F at George AFB and who were unused to the European weather and airspace restrictions. On 11 April 1975, JBG 35 at Pferdsfeld flew its last Fiat G.91 sorties and began conversion to the F-4F.

In 1982, the RF-4Es were given a secondary ground-attack role and were updated with improved sensors (such as IR linescan) and an

F-4D-35-MC 3-602 (67-14870) of the IIAF's 306th FS, is shown fitted with a ventral gun pod at Mehrabad in August 1969. This aircraft was one of an initial order for 16 F-4Ds, subsequent orders for 16 F-4Ds, 208 F-4Es and 32 RF-4Es being received, although the last 31 F-4Es and 16 RF-4Es were cancelled by the US government after the overthrow of the Shah in 1979. *(McDonnell Douglas)*

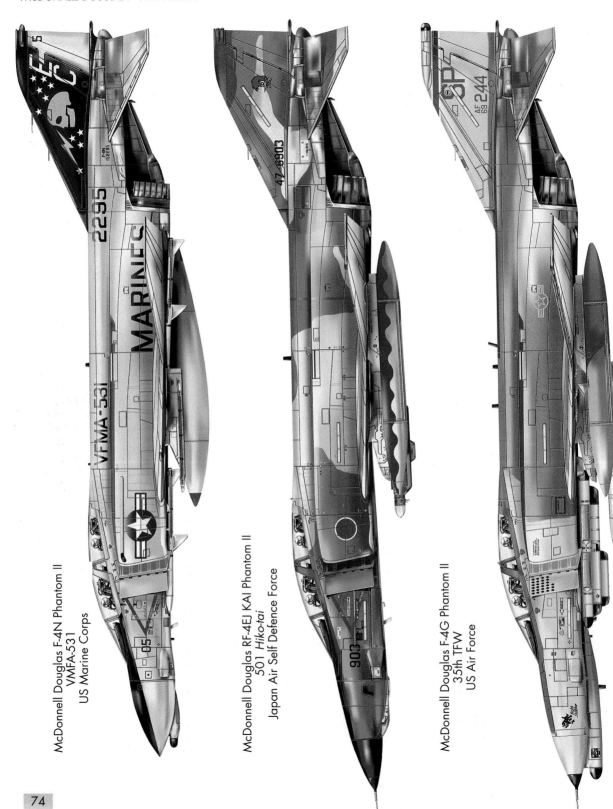

McDonnell Douglas F-4N Phantom II
VMFA-531
US Marine Corps

McDonnell Douglas RF-4EJ KAI Phantom II
501 *Hiko-tai*
Japan Air Self Defence Force

McDonnell Douglas F-4G Phantom II
35th TFW
US Air Force

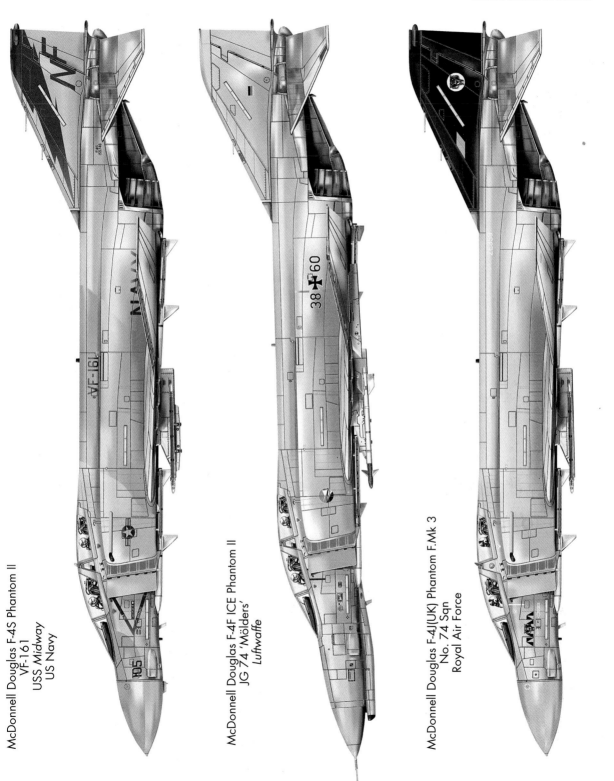

McDonnell Douglas F-4S Phantom II
VF-161
USS Midway
US Navy

McDonnell Douglas F-4F ICE Phantom II
JG 74 'Mölders'
Luftwaffe

McDonnell Douglas F-4J(UK) Phantom F.Mk 3
No. 74 Sqn
Royal Air Force

Above: F-4B-19-MC BuNo. 151485 of VF-21 'Freelancers', from the USS *Midway*, uses standard dive-bombing technique against a North Vietnamese target. The bombs are 500-lb (227-kg) Mk 82 Snakeyes, with retarding fins that pop out after launch. *(USN)*

Left: This 106th TRS, 117th RW RF-4C of the Alabama ANG, carries Gulf War mission markings. During Operation *Desert Shield* in 1990, six RF-4Cs were used on cross-border reconnaissance missions from Sheikh Isa, Bahrain, using LOROP. During *Desert Storm*, early in 1991, they flew day tactical reconnaissance missions, including searches for mobile 'Scud' missile launchers, as part of America's tactical reconnaissance effort. *(Author)*

F-4B-15-MC BuNo. 152227 of VF-114 'Aardvarks', pictured as it lands aboard the USS *Kitty Hawk* during operations in the South China Sea. *(USN)*

F-4B-14-MC BuNo. 150487 of XF-3 Air Test and Evaluation Squadron, minus its fin-tip antenna, launches from a carrier on 20 March 1967. *(McDonnell Douglas)*

Above: In January 1969, seven modified F-4Js were assigned to the USN's 'Blue Angels' demonstration team. The team made its debut with the type at MCAS Yuma, Arizona, on 15 March 1969, and for five seasons thrilled millions worldwide with its precision F-4 flying. The 'Blues' flew the F-4J until the end of the 1973 season, when the energy crisis forced a change to the A-4F Skyhawk. (McDonnell Douglas)

Project *High Jump* F4H-1 BuNo. 149449 being flown on 3 April 1962, when, over NAS Point Mugu, Lt-Cdr John W. Young, USN climbed to 25000 m (82,021 ft) in 230.44 seconds. In 1962, eight separate altitude records were set by F4H-1s during Project *High Jump*. (McDonnell Douglas)

Above: TAC F-4Es equipped the USAF Air Demonstration Squadron (the 4510th ADS), the 'Thunderbirds', at Nellis AFB for five years. After converting from F-100Ds, the 'Thunderbirds' made their debut in F-4Es at the Air Force Academy in Colorado Springs, Colorado, on 4 June 1969. Rising fuel costs forced the 'Thunderbirds' to convert to Northrop T-38A Talons in 1974.

Top: F-4B-22-MC Phantoms of VMFA-323 'Death Rattlers' taxi out at Da Nang, South Vietnam in June 1966. The nearest aircraft is BuNo. 152258/WS-6. *(both McDonnell Douglas)*

Above: F-4D-29-MC 66-0234 and F-4D-28-MC 65-0705, of the 433rd and 435th TFSs, 8th TFW 'Wolfpack', armed with GBU-10A Paveway I LGBs, were flying out of Ubon RTAFB, Thailand, to targets in North Vietnam in 1970. The 'Wolfpack' moved to Kunsan AB at the end of the war in South-East Asia, flying the F-4D until September 1981, when it re-equipped with the F-16A. *(USAF via Thomas J. Fitton)*

Below: F-4D-32-MC 66-8747 hailed from PACAF's 3rd TFW at Clark AFB in the Philippines. The bulged fairing under the nose radome contains the pre-amplifier and antennas for the APR-25/26 RHAWS. *(via Matthias Vogelsang)*

F-4D-30-MC 66-7548, one of 18 loaned to the RoKAF as part of the *Peace Spectator* programme to replace F-86Ds with the 1st FW. *(McDonnell Douglas)*

optical sight. JG 71's and JG 74's F-4Fs were modernised in the early 1990s under the ICE programme. Both JBG 35's and JBG 36's F-4Fs also received upgrades. Some German Phantoms were replaced by Tornados.

Australia

In March 1963, the Australian Government ordered 24 F-111C variable-geometry strike and reconnaissance aircraft in preference to the Model 98-DX (F-4C), to replace its Australian-built Canberra B.Mk 20 bombers. This was disappointing for McDonnell Douglas, which had included French-built SNECMA Atar 9 engines in its proposal, on the basis that these engines already powered the Royal Australian Air Force (RAAF) Dassault Mirage IIICs. The delivery of the F-111Cs was scheduled for 1968, but the onset of fatigue problems with the F-111 in the US would seriously delay service entry, leaving the RAAF without attack aircraft. On 22 June 1970 therefore, the US agreed to divert 24 F-4Es (69-7201/7217, 69-7219/7220, 69-7304/ 7307 and 69-7324) from USAF production contracts for an initial two-year lease at a cost of $34 million inclusive of spares and ground support equipment. These aircraft equipped Nos 1 and 6 Sqns of No. 82 (Bomber) Wing at Amberley, Brisbane, between September 1970 and 1973, when the F-111Cs were finally delivered. Late in 1972, 11 of the F-4Es (one was

This IDF/AF F-4E has had its markings obliterated by the censor. *(IDF/AF)*

lost in an accident off New South Wales in June 1971) were returned to the USAF with the last 12 leaving Australia in June 1973.

Spain

In 1971 the *Ejército del Aire Español* (Spanish air force or EdA) sought to replace its F-104Gs with the F-4C. From October 1971 to September 1972, the EdA received 36 F-4Cs from USAFE's 81st TFW. Each aircraft (some of which had already been used in the war in South-East Asia) was completely overhauled at the Construcciones Aeronauticas SA (CASA) plant at Getafe and delivered to the EdA with the Spanish designation C.12. All were used to equip the newly commissioned *Escuadrón* 121 at Torrejón,

RAAF F-4E-43-MC Phantoms 97213, 97214 and 97209 (69-7213, 69-7214 and 69-7209, respectively) in formation over Australia in March 1971. Twenty-four F-4Es were loaned to Australia to equip Nos 1 and 6 Sqns, RAAF at Amberley, Brisbane. The survivors were returned to the USA late in June 1973 and all were among the aircraft converted to F-4G Wild Weasel configuration for the USAF. (RAAF)

and later Esc 122 (after Esc 104 disbanded). Four F-4Cs were lost in accidents and were replaced, in July and August 1978, by ex-USAF F-4Cs from the 35th TFW and 58th Tactical Training Wing (TTW). Four RF-4Cs arrived from October to November 1978 and were designated CR.12 in EdA service.

During the winter of 1988, the C.12s of Esc 121 and Esc 122 at Torrejón were replaced by the C.15 (EF-l8 Hornet). In January 1989, eight ex-Kentucky ANG RF-4Cs arrived to join the four original CR.12s to enable the EdA to form a specialised tactical reconnaissance squadron. The CR.12s remained in service until the late 1990s.

Japan

Reductions in Japanese defence expenditure between 1965 and 1970 prevented development of a new, indigenous fighter known as the F-X, so Japan successfully negotiated for licence-production of the Phantom. In July 1971, two McDonnell Douglas-built F-4EJ pattern prototype aircraft were delivered and during the Fourth Defence Build-up Program (DBP), orders were placed with Mitsubishi Heavy Industries at Nagoya for 128 production aircraft for the JASDF. Eleven F-4EJs were also assembled in Japan. After evaluation by the *Koku Jikkendan* (Air Proving Wing) at Komaki, F-4EJs were

assigned on 1 August 1972 to the *Rinji* (Provisional) 301 *Hiko-tai* (Squadron) as part of 7 *Koku-dan* (Air Wing) at Nyutabaru. In October 1973, 301 *Hiko-tai* became a fully fledged squadron in 5 *Koku-dan*. F-4EJs were assigned to four other *Hiko-tais*; 302 in 7 *Koku-dan* at Naha, 303 of 6 *Koku-dan* at Komatsu, 304 at Tsuiki in 8 *Koku-dan* and, in 1977, 305 at Hyakuri on Okinawa as part of the S-W Mixed Air Wing. Upgraded F-4EJ KAIs entered service with 306 *Hiko-tai* in November 1989. In November 1974, 14 McDonnell Douglas-built RF-4EJs were assigned to the 501 *Hiko-tai* of the *Teisatsu Koku-tai* (Tactical Reconnaissance Group) at Hyakuri.

Greece

In March 1974 the *Elliniki Aeroporia* (Hellenic air force (HAF)) took delivery of 38 F-4Es under *Peace Icarus* for service in 338 and 339 *Mira* (squadrons) of the 117 *Pterix Mahis* (Combat Wing), 28th *Taktiki Aeroporiki Dynamis* (Tactical Air Force) at Andravida. Two replacement aircraft were received in 1975 to make good two losses and eight RF-4Es were received for 348

These aircraft are C.12 Phantoms of the EdA, which received 36 ex-USAF F-4Cs between October 1971 and September 1972, with four more arriving between July and August 1978. The C.12s equipped Esc 121 and Esc 122 of Ala 12 at Torrejón, until the winter of 1988. *(McDonnell Douglas)*

Altogether, Mitsubishi Heavy Industries Ltd built 127 F-4EJs under licence. Here F-4EJs 67-8378 and 67-8368 are illustrated. *(McDonnell Douglas)*

Mira Taktikis Anagnoriseos of 110 *Pterix Mahis* at Larissa. In 1977, President Carter sanctioned the sale of 18 more F-4Es for delivery in 1978–79. In 1988, 69 ex-AFRES and ANG F-4Cs and F-4Ds were acquired by the HAF.

Turkey

Beginning in August 1974, 72 F-4Es were delivered to the *Türk Hava Kuvvetleri* (THK, or Turkish air force) under *Peace Diamond III* and *IV*. These were for the fighter-strike role within NATO's 6th Allied Tactical Air Force, equipping 113 *Filo* (squadron) of the *Birinci Taktik Hava*

During 1974–76, Greece received 38 F-4Es (and two additional aircraft as attrition replacements) for its air force. These were followed (1978–79) by a further 18 F-4E aircraft. *(HAF)*

Kuvveti Komutanligi (1st Tactical Air Force Command) at Eskisehir and 162 Filo at Bandirma. They also equipped the 111 and 112 *Filoler* (squadrons) at Eskisehir; the 131 and 132 *Filoler* at Konya; and the 171, 172 and 173 *Filoler* at Erhac in *Ikinci Taktik Hava Kuvveti Komutanligi* (2nd Tactical Air Force Command). In 1977, the US Government approved the export of 32 more F-4Es and eight RF-4Es and by 1988 the THK had obtained 45 ex-USAF F-4Es. Additional F-4Es

This THK F-4E was one of 72 new F-4Es (and eight RF-4Es) delivered to Turkey under *Peace Diamond III* and *IV* beginning in August 1974. *(McDonnell Douglas)*

from surplus US stocks followed during the late 1980s and early 1990s.

Egypt

In 1980 the *Al Quwwat al Jawwiya il Misriya* (Arab Republic of Egypt Air Force) received 35 early production, ex-USAF F-4Es under the *Peace Pharaoh* programme, to re-equip two squadrons in the 222nd Tactical Fighter Brigade at Cairo-West. Unfortunately, the Phantoms, which had already seen considerable service, proved too difficult to maintain and in May 1982 they were flown back to the USA for major overhaul and reassignment to another air force. However, Egypt had a change of heart since plans were by now well advanced to equip the Arab Republic of Egypt Air Force with 120 F-16 Fighting Falcons and 120 F-5G Tigersharks. The F-4Es therefore remained in service with the two squadrons of the 222nd Fighter Regiment at Cairo-West until replacement by the newer types.

Appendix 1. Weapons and Stores: F-4A/F-4B–F-4E Phantom

The Phantom featured nine stores stations as follows: **Station 1:** Underwing pylon, outboard, port wing (inboard of fold); **2:** Underwing pylon, inboard, port wing; **3:** Recessed in rear fuselage, port side; **4:** Recessed in front fuselage, port side; **5:** Fuselage centreline; **6:** Recessed in front fuselage, starboard side; **7:** Recessed in rear fuselage, starboard side; **8:** Underwing pylon, inboard, starboard wing; **9:** Underwing pylon, outboard, starboard wing (inboard of fold). The following stores could be carried by the F-4A–F-4E:

Quantity	Weight	Nominal weight	Store
2	106 kg (234 lb) (empty)		370-US gal (1400.5-litre) wing drop tank
1	235 lb (empty)		600-US gal (2271-litre) centreline drop tank
4	70.3 kg (155 lb)		AIM-9B Sidewinder (Sidewinder 1A) AAM
4	92.5 kg (204 lb)		AIM-9C Sidewinder (Sidewinder 1C) AAM
			AIM-4D Falcon AAM (F-4D only)
6	182/206 kg (402/455 lb)		AIM-7D/E Sparrow (Sparrow III) AAM
4	181 kg (400 lb)		AGM-45A Shrike ARM
2	263.1 kg (580 lb)		AGM-12B Bullpup
2	806.5 kg (1,778 lb)		AGM-I2C Bullpup
15	78.5 kg (173 lb)		LAU-32A/A rocket launcher
15	193.7 kg (427 lb)		LAU-3A/A rocket launcher
15	241.8 kg (533 lb)		LAU-10/A rocket launcher
3	805.1 kg (1,775 lb)		SUU-16/A M61 20-mm gun pod
1	611.5 kg (1,348 lb)		Mk 4 20-mm gun pod
15	147.4 kg (325 lb)		SUU-31/A 7.62-mm (0.3-in) gun pod
9	117.9 kg (260 lb)	250 lb	Mk 81 general-purpose bomb
24	240.9 kg (531 lb)	500 lb	Mk 82 general purpose bomb
11	446.8 kg (985 lb)	1,000 lb	Mk 83 general-purpose bomb
24	133.8 kg (295 lb)	250 lb	Mk 81 Snakeye retarded bomb
24	254 kg (560 lb)	500 lb	Mk 82 Snakeye retarded bomb
5	204.6 kg (451 lb)		SUU-20 practice bomb/rocket dispenser
1	282.1 kg (622 lb)		SUU-21/A practice bomb dispenser
13	340.2 kg (750 lb)		CBU-75 Sadeye cluster bomb
11	326.6 kg (720 lb)		MC-1 chemical bomb
24	240.4 kg (530 lb)		Mk 116 Weteye chemical bomb
18	99.8 kg (220-lb)		M129E1 leaflet bomb
1	925 kg (2,040 lb)		Mk 28 MOD 1 FF nuclear weapon (fuselage centreline)

Quantity	Weight	Nominal weight	Store
1	934.4 kg (2,060 lb)		Mk 43 MOD 0 nuclear weapon (fuselage centreline)
1	226.8 kg (500 lb)		Mk 57 nuclear weapon (fuselage centreline)
2	352 kg (776 lb)		AB45Y-1 spray tank
15	254 kg (560 lb)		Mk 12 Smoke Tank 220
11	372 kg (820 lb)	750 lb	M117 general-purpose bomb
15	299.4 kg (660 lb)		MLU-10/B landmine
11	314.8 kg (694 lb) (full)		BLU-1/B napalm bomb (416.4 litre; 110 US gal)
11	310.7 kg (685 lb) (full)		M116A2 napalm bomb (416.4 litre; 110 US gal)
24	235.9 kg (520 lb)		Mk 77 napalm bomb
13	413.7 kg (912 lb)		Mk 79 napalm bomb
22	115.7 kg (225 lb)		Fireye napalm bomb
7	339.7 kg (749 lb)		CBU-1A/A cluster bomb
7	376.5 kg (830 lb)		CBU-2A/A cluster bomb
19	360.6 kg (795 lb)		CBU-7/A cluster bomb
5	39.5 kg (87 lb)		Practice Multiple Bomb Rack A/A37R –3
1	81.6 kg (180 lb)		QRC-160 ECM pod

In addition to the above the F-4E could additionally carry the following weapons:

Quantity	Weight	Nominal weight	Store
4	197.3 kg (435 lb)		AIM-7E-2 Sparrow AAM
8	421.8 kg (930 lb)		M36E2 incendiary bomb
16	399.2 kg (880 lb)	750 lb	M117D destruction weapon and M117RE retarded bomb
1	1369.9 kg (3,020 lb)	3,000 lb	M118 general-purpose bomb (fuselage centreline)
17	326.6 kg (720 lb)		MC-1 gas bomb
11	392.4 kg (865 lb)		BLU-1/B and -1B/B unfinned fire bomb
11	385.6 kg (850 lb)		BLU-27B and -27A/B unfinned fire bomb
4	393.7 kg (868 lb)		BLU-27B and -27A/B finned fire bomb
4	362.9 kg (800 lb)		BLU-52/B finned fire bomb
3	1179.4 kg (2,600 lb)		BLU-76 fire bomb
10	68.9 kg (152 lb)		MLU-32/B99 (Briteye) flare dispenser
4	92.1 kg (203 lb)		QRC-160A-1/ALQ-71 ECM pod
4	83.9 kg (185 lb)		QRC-160A-2/ALQ-72 ECM pod
4	122 kg (269 lb)		QRC-160A-8/ALQ-87 ECM pod
4	178.3 kg (393 lb)		QRC-335A(V)-3/ALQ-101 ECM pod
4	212.3 kg (468 lb)		QRC-335A(V)-4/ALQ-101 ECM pod
2	872.3 kg (1,923 lb)		TMU-28B or PAU-7/A spray tank
1	680.4 kg (1,500 lb)		A/A 37U-15 tow target
1			RMU-8/A tow target
2			AVQ-10 Pave Knife pod
5			AAVS IV camera pod
4	930.8 kg (2,052 lb)		KMU-351/B (Mk 84LGB) LGB
4	1037.8 kg (2,288 lb)		KMU-353A/B (Mk 84EO) EO- guided bomb
4	963 kg (2,123 lb)		KMU-359/B (Mk 841R) guided bomb
2	1370 kg (3,020 lb)		KMU-370A/B (Mk 118LGB) LGB
2	1564.9 kg (3,450 lb)		KMU-390/B (Mk 118EO) EO- guided bomb

Appendix 2. Production Details

Model	Block	Service	BuNo./Serial	Quantity
YF4H-1		USN	142259/142260	2
F-4A	1	USN	143388/143392	5
	2	USN	145307/145317	11
	3	USN	146817/146821	5
	4	USN	148252/148261	10
	5	USN	148262/148275	14
F-4B	6	USN	148363/148386	24
	7	USN	148387/148410	24
	8	USN	148411/148434	24
	9	USN	149403/149426	24
	10	USN	149427/149450	24
	11	USN	149451/149474	24
	12	USN	150408/150435	30
	13	USN	150438/150479	44
	14	USN	150480/150493	
		USN	150624/10851	42
	15	USN	150652/10653	
		USN	150993/151021	
		USN	151397/151398	33
	16	USN	151399/151426	28
	17	USN	151427/151447	21
	18	USN	151448/151472	25
	19	USN	151473/151497	25
	20	USN	151498/151519	
		USN	152207/152215	31
	21	USN	152216/152243	28
	22	USN	152244/152272	29
	23	USN	152273/152304	32
	24	USN	152305/152331	27
	25	USN	152965/152994	30
	26	USN	152995/153029	35
	27	USN	153030/153058	27
	28	USN	153057/153070	
		USN	153912/150915	18
RF-4B	20	USMC	151975/151977	3
	21	USMC	151978/151979	2
	22	USMC	151980/151981	2
	23	USMC	151982/151983	2
	24	USMC	153089/153094	6

Model	Block	Service	BuNo./Serial	Quantity
RF-4B	25	USMC	163095/153100	6
	26	USMC	153101/153107	7
	27	USMC	153108/153115	8
	41	USMC	157342/157346	5
	43	USMC	157347/157351	5
F-4C	15	USAF	62-12199	
		USAF	63-7407/7420	15
	16	USAF	63-7421/7442	22
	17	USAF	63-7443/7468	26
	18	USAF	63-7469/7526	58
	19	USAF	63-7527/7597	71
	20	USAF	63-7598/7662	65
	21	USAF	63-7663/7713	
		USAF	64-0654/0664	70
	22	USAF	64-0673/0737	65
	23	USAF	64-0738/0817	80
	24	USAF	64-0818/0881	64
	25	USAF	64-0882/0928	47
RF-4C	14	USAF	62-12200/12201	2
	17	USAF	63-7740/7742	3
	18	USAF	63-7743/7749	7
	19	USAF	63-7750/7763	14
	20	USAF	64-0997/1017	21
	21	USAF	64-1018/1037	20
	22	USAF	64-1038/1061	24
	23	USAF	64-1062/1077	16
	24	USAF	64-1078/1085	
		USAF	65-0818/0838	29
	25	USAF	65-0839/0864	26
	26	USAF	65-0865/0901	37
	27	USAF	65-0902/0932	31
	28	USAF	65-0933/0945	
		USAF	66-0383/0386	
		USAF	66-0388	18
	29	USAF	66-0387	
		USAF	66-0389/0406	19
	30	USAF	66-0407/0428	22
	31	USAF	66-0429/0450	22
	32	USAF	66-0451/0472	22

Model	Block	Service	BuNo./Serial	Quantity
RF-4C	33	USAF	66-0473/0478	
		USAF	67-0428/0442	21
	34	USAF	67-0443/0453	11
	35	USAF	67-0454/0461	8
	36	USAF	67-0462/0469	8
	37	USAF	68-0548/0561	14
	38	USAF	68-0562/0676	15
	39	USAF	68-0577/0593	17
	40	USAF	68-0594/0611	18
	41	USAF	69-0349/0357	9
	42	USAF	69-0358/0366	9
	43	USAF	69-0367/0375	9
	44	USAF	69-0376/0384	9
	48	USAF	71-0248/0252	5
	49	USAF	71-0253/0259	7
	51	USAF	72-0145/0150	6
	52	USAF	72-0151/0153	3
	53	USAF	72-0154/0156	3
F-4D	24	USAF	64-0929/0937	9
	25	USAF	64-0938/0963	26
	26	USAF	64-0964/0980	
		USAF	65-0580/0611	49
	27	USAF	65-0612/0665	54
	28	USAF	65-0666/0770	105
	29	USAF	65-0771/0801	
		USAF	66-7455/7504	132
	30	USAF	66-7505/7650	146
	31	USAF	66-7651/7774	
		USAF	66-8685/8698	138
	32	USAF	66-8699/8786	88
	33	USAF	66-8787/8825	32
	35	IIAF	67-14869/14876	8
	36	IIAF	67-14877/14884	8
	37	IIAF	68-6904/6911	8
	38	IIAF	68-6912/6919	8
F-4E	31	USAF	66-0284/0297	14
	32	USAF	66-0298/0338	41
	33	USAF	66-0339/0382	
		USAF	67-0208/0219	56
	34	USAF	67-0220/0282	63
	35	USAF	67-0283/0341	59
	36	USAF	67-0342/0398	57
	37	USAF	68-0303/0365	63
	38	USAF	68-0366/0395	
		USAF	68-0400/0409	40
	39	USAF	68-0410/0413	
		USAF	68-0418/0433	
		USAF	68-0438/0451	34
	40	USAF	68-0452/0453	
		USAF	68-0458/0468	
		USAF	68-0473/0483	
		USAF	68-0488/0494	31
	41	USAF	68-0495/0498	
		USAF	68-0503/0518	
		USAF	68-0526/0538	33
F-4E	42	USAF	69-0236/0303	68
	43	USAF	69-0304/0307	
		USAF	69-7201/7260	64
	44	USAF	69-7261/7273	
		USAF	69-7286/7303	
		USAF	69-7546/7578	64
	45	USAF	69-7579/7589	11
	48	USAF	71-0224/0247	24
	49	USAF	71-1070/1093	24
	50	USAF	71-1391/1402	
		USAF	72-0121/0138	38
	51	USAF	72-0139/0144	
		USAF	72-0157/0159	9
	52	USAF	72-0160/0165	6
	53	USAF	72-0166/0168	
		USAF	72-1407	4
	54	USAF	72-1476/1489	14
	55	USAF	72-1490/1497	8
	56	USAF	72-1498/1499	2
	57	USAF	73-1157/1164	8
	58	USAF	73-1165/1184	20
	59	USAF	73-1185/1204	20
	60	USAF	74-0643/0666	
		USAF	74-1038/1049	36
	61	USAF	74-1050/1061	
		USAF	74-1620/1637	30
	62	USAF	74-1638/1653	16
	63	USAF/Luftwaffe	75-0628/0637	12
	38	IDF/AF	68-0396/0399	4
	39	IDF/AF	68-0414/0417	
		IDF/AF	68-0434/0437	8
	40	IDF/AF	68-0454/0457	
		IDF/AF	68-0469/0472	12
		IDF/AF	68-0484/0487	
	41	IDF/AF	68-0499/0502	
		IDF/AF	68-0519/0525	
		IDF/AF	68-0539/0547	20
	46	IIAF	69-7711/7726	16
	47	IIAF	69-7727/7742	16
	51	IDF/AF	71-1779/1786	8
		IIAF	71-1094/1101	8
	52	IIAF	71-1102/1115	14
		IDF/AF	71-1787/1793	7
	53	IIAF	71-1116/1129	14
		IDF/AF	71-1794/1796	3
	54	IIAF	71-1130/1142	13
		HAF	72-1500/1507	8
	55	IIAF	71-1143/1152	10
		HAF	72-1508/1523	16
	56	THK	73-1016/1027	12
		HAF	72-1524/1535	12
		IIAF	71-1153/1166	14
	57	THK	73-1028/1042	15
		IIAF	73-1519/1534	16

Model	Block	Service	BuNo./Serial	Quantity
F-4E	58	THK	73-1043/1055	13
		IIAF	73-1535/1549	15
	59	IIAF	73-1550/1554	5
	60	IDF/AF	74-1014/1015	2
		HAF	74-1618/1619	2
	61	IDF/AF	74-1016/102	16
	62	IDF/AF	74-1022/1037	16
	63	IIAF	75-0222/0257	36
	64	RoKAF	76-0493/0511	19
	65	THK	77-0277/0300	24
		HAF	77-1743/1750	8
	66	THK	77-0301/0308	8
		HAF	77-1751/1760	10
	67	RoKAF	78-0727/0744	18
F-4EJ (US-built)	45	JASDF	17-8301/8302	
		JASDF	27-8303/8306	
		JASDF	37-8307/8310	10
	47	JASDF	37-8311/8313	3
F-4EJ (Japan-built)		JASDF	37-8314/8323	10
		JASDF	47-8324/8352	29
		JASDF	57-8353/8376	24
		JASDF	67-8377/8391	15
		JASDF	77-8392/8403	12
		JASDF	87-8404/8415	12
		JASDF	97-8416/8427	12
		JASDF	07-8428/8436	9
		JASDF	17-8437/8440	4
RF-4E	43	Luftwaffe	3501/3508	8
	44	Luftwaffe	3509/3515	7
	45	Luftwaffe	3516/3534	19
		IDF/AF	69-7590/7595	6
	46	Luftwaffe	3535/3563	29
	47	Luftwaffe	3564/3588	25
	48	IIAF	72-0266/0269	4
	61	IIAF	74-1725/1728	4
	62	IIAF	74-1729/1736	8
	63	IDF/AF	75-0418/0423	6
	66	THK	77-0309/0316	8
		HAF	77-0357/0358	
		HAF	77-1761/1766	8
RF-4EJ	56	JASDF	47-6901/6905	5
	57	JASDF	57-6906/6914	9
F-4F	52	Luftwaffe	3701/3709	9
	53	Luftwaffe	3710/3724	15
	54	Luftwaffe	3725/3748	24
	55	Luftwaffe	3749/3772	24
	56	Luftwaffe	3773/3796	24
	57	Luftwaffe	3797/3820	24
	58	Luftwaffe	3821/3844	24
	59	Luftwaffe	3845/3875	31
F-4J	26	USN	163071/153075	5
	27	USN	153076/153088	13
	28	USN	153768/153779	12
	29	USN	153780/153799	20
	30	USN	153800/153839	40

Model	Block	Service	BuNo./Serial	Quantity
F-4J	31	USN	153840/153876	37
	32	USN	153877/153911	
		USN	154781/154785	40
	33	USN	154786/154788	
		USN	155504/155569	69
	34	USN	155570/155580	
		USN	155731/155784	65
	35	USN	155785/155843	59
	36	USN	155844/155866	23
	37	USN	155867/155874	8
	38	USN	155875/155889	15
	39	USN	155890/155902	13
	40	USN	157242/157260	19
	41	USN	157261/157273	13
	42	USN	155903	
		USN	157274/157285	13
	43	USN	157286/157297	12
	44	USN	157298/157309	12
	45	USN	158346/158354	9
	46	USN	158355/158365	11
	47	USN	158366/158379	14
YF-4K	26	RN	XT595/XT596	2
F-4K*	27	RN	XT597/XT598	2
	30	RN	XT857/XT858	2
	31	RN	XT859/XT862	4
	32	RN	XT863/XT870	8
	33	RN	XT871/XT876	6
	34	RN	XV565/XV571	7
	35	RN	XV572/XV578	7
	36	RN	XV579/XV585	7
	37	RN	XV586/XV592	7
YF-4M	29	RAF	XT852/XT853	2
F-4M**	31	RAF	XT891/XT895	5
	32	RAF	XT896/XT906	11
	33	RAF	XT907/XT914	14
		RAF	XV393/XV398	14
	34	RAF	XV399/XV417	19
	35	RAF	XV418/XV436	19
	36	RAF	XV437/XV442	
		RAF	XV460/XV475	22
	37	RAF	XV476/XV495	20
	38	RAF	XV496/XV501	6

*14 aircraft were diverted to the RAF F-4M contract
**130 aircraft in total, although only 118 were delivered

Totals

Model	Notes	Subtotals
F-4A		45
F-4B		649
RF-4B		46
F-4C		583
RF-4C		505
F-4D	793 for USAF/32 for export	825
F-4E	952 for USAF/428 for export	1,380
F-4EJ		13

Model	Notes	Subtotals
F-4EJ*		127
RF-4E		132
RF-4EJ		14
F-4F		175
F-4J		522
F-4K		52
F-4M		118
Grand Total		**5,195**
Total by McDonnell Douglas		**5,068**

*built by Mitsubishi

Appendix 3. Specifications

Parameter	F-4B	F-4J	RF-4C	F-4E	F-4M
Wing span	11.71 m (38 ft 4⅞ in)	11.71 m (38 ft 4⅞ in)	11.71 m (38 ft 4⅞ in)	11.71 m (38 ft 4⅞ in)	11.71 m (38 ft 4⅞ in)
Wing span, folded	8.41 m (27 ft 7 in)	8.41 m (27 ft 7 in)	8.41 m (27 ft 7 in)	8.41 m (27 ft 7 in)	8.41 m (27 ft 7 in)
Length	17.77 m (58 ft 3¾ in)	17.77 m (58 ft 3¾ in)	19.17 m (62 ft 10⅞ in)	19.20 m (63 ft)	17.55 m (57 ft 7 in)
Height	4.95 m (16 ft 3 in)	4.82 m (15 ft 8½ in)	5.03 m (16 ft 6 in)	5.03 m (16 ft 6 in)	4.90 m (16 ft 1 in)
Wing area	49.24 m² (530 sq ft)	49.24 m² (530 sq ft)	49.24 m² (530 sq ft)	49.24 m² (530 sq ft)	49.24 m² (530 sq ft)
Empty weight	12654 kg (27,897 lb)	13961 kg (30,778 lb)	12826 kg (28,276 lb)	13397 kg (29,535 lb)	14061 kg (31,000 lb)
Loaded weight	19916 kg (43,907 lb)	23300 kg (51,268 lb)	22834 kg (50,341 lb)	25382 kg (55,957 lb)	23,768 kg (5,400 lb)
Maximum weight	24766 kg (54,600 lb)	25401 kg (56,001 lb)	26308 kg (58,100 lb)	27965 kg (61,651 lb)	25401 kg (56,000 lb)
Maximum speed (speed/at altitude)	2389 km/h/ 14630 m (1,485 mph/ 48,000 ft)	2298 km/h/ 11000 m (1,428 mph/ 36,100 ft)	2348 km/h/ 12190 m (1,459 mph/ 40,000 ft)	2389 km/h/ 12190 m (1,485 mph/ 40,000 ft)	2231 km/h/ 12190 m (1,386 mph/ 40,000 ft)
Cruising speed	925 km/h (575 mph)	907 km/h (564 mph)	945 km/h (587 mph)	941 km/h (585 mph)	
Climb rate	207 m/s (40,800 ft/min)	210 m/s (41,250 ft/min)	245 m/s (48,300 ft/min)	312 m/s (61,400 ft/min)	163 m/s (32,000 ft/min)
Service ceiling	18900 m (62,000 ft)	16675 m (54,700 ft)	18105 m (59,400 ft)	18975 m (62,250 ft)	18530 m (60,800 ft)
Normal range	2590 km (1,610 miles)	2220 km (1,380 miles)	2210 km (1,375 miles)	1690 km (1,050 miles)	1610 km (1,000 miles)
Maximum range	4705 km (2,925 miles)	2815 km (1,750 miles)	2815 km (1,750 miles)	3035 km (1,885 miles)	2815 km (1,750 miles)

Appendix 4. US Phantom Units

US Air Force

Air Force Logistics Command

Unit	Location	Model
Ogden ALC	Ogden AFB, UH	F-4C, RF-4C

Air Force Systems Command

Unit	Location	Model
3246th TW	Eglin AFB, FL	F-4C, F-4D, F-4E
6512nd TS	Edwards AFB, CA	RF-4C, F-4D, F-4E

Pacific Air Forces

Unit	Location	Model
3rd TFW	Clark AB, Philippines	F-4E, F-4G
18th TFW	Kadena AB, Okinawa	RF-4C
51st TFW	Osan AB, Korea	F-4E

Tactical Air Command

Unit	Location	Model
4th TFW	Seymour Johnson AFB, NC	F-4E
31st TFW	Homestead AFB, FL	F-4D
35th TFW	George AFB, CA	F-4E
37th TFW	George AFB, CA	F-4E, F-4G
57th FWW	Nellis AFB, NV	F-4E
67th TRW	Bergstrom AFB, TX	RF-4C
347th TFW	Moody AFB, GA	F-4E
363rd TFW	Shaw AFB, SC	RF-4C
57th FIS	Keflavik AB, Iceland	F-4E
4485th TS	Eglin AFB, FL	F-4E, F-4G

US Air Forces in Europe

Unit	Location	Model
10th TRW	RAF Alconbury, UK	RF-4C
26th TRW	Zweibrücken AB, West Germany	RF-4C
52nd TFW	Spangdahlem AB, West Germany	F-4E, F-4G
86th TFW	Ramstein AB, West Germany	F-4E
401st TFW	Torrejón AB, Spain	F-4D

Air Force Reserve

Unit	Location	Model
89th TFS, 906th TFG	Dayton, OH	F-4D
93rd TFS, 482nd TFW	Homestead AFB, FL	F-4D
457th TFS, 301st TFW	Carswell AFB, TX	F-4D
465th TFS, 507th TFG	Tinker AFB, OK	F-4D
704th TFS, 924th TFG	Bergstrom AFB, TX	F-4D

Air National Guard

Unit	Location	Model
106th TRS, 117 TRW	Birmingham, AL	RF-4C
110th TFS, 131st TFW	St Louis, MO	F-4C
111th FIS, 147th FIG	Ellington AFB, TX	F-4C
113th TFS, 181st TFG	Terre Haute, IN	F-4C
121st TFS, 113th TFW	Andrews AFB, MD	F-4D
522nd TFS, 159th TFG	NAS New Orleans, LA	F-4C
123rd FIS, 142nd FIG	Portland, OR	F-4C
127th TFTS, 184th TFTG	McConnell AFB, KS	F-4D
128th TFS, 116th TFW	Dobbins AFB, GA	F-4D
134th TFS, 158th TFG	Burlington, VT	F-4D
136th FIS, 107th FIG	Niagara Falls, NY	F-4C
141st TFS, 108th TFW	McGuire AFB, NJ	F-4D
153rd TRS, 186th TRG	Meridian, MS	RF-4C
160th TRS, 187th TRG	Montgomery, AL	RF-4C
163rd TFS, 122nd TFW	Fort Wayne, IN	F-4C
165th TRS, 123rd TRW	Louisville, KY	RF-4C
170th TFS, 183rd TFG	Springfield, IN	F-4D
171st FIS, 191st FIG	Selfridge, MI	F-4C
173rd TRS, 155th TRG	Lincoln, NE	RF-4C
178th FIS, 119th FIG	Fargo, ND	F-4D
179th TRS, 148th TRG	Duluth, MN	RF-4C
182nd TFS, 149th TFG	Kelly AFB, TX	F-4C
184th TFS, 188th TFG	Fort Smith, AR	F-4C
190th TRS, 124th TRG	Boise, ID	RF-4C
192nd TRS, 152nd TRG	Reno, NV	RF-4C
196th TFS, 163rd TFG	March AFB, CA	F-4C
199th FIS, 154 TFG	Hickam AFB, HI	F-4C

US Navy

Squadron	Traditional home port
VF-11 'Red Rippers'	NAS Oceana, VA
VF-14 'Tophatters'	NAS Oceana, VA
VR-21 'Freelancers'	NAS Miramar, CA
VF-22L1	NAS Alameda, CA
VF-31 'Tomcatters'	NAS Oceana, VA
VF-32 'Swordsmen'	NAS Oceana, VA
VF-33 'Tarsiers'	NAS Ocean, VA
VF-41 'Black Aces'	NAS Miramar, CA
VF-51 'Screaming Eagles'	NAS Miramar, CA
VF-74 'Bedevilers'	NAS Oceana, VA
VF-84 'Jolly Rogers'	NAS Oceana, VA
VF-92 'Silver Kites'	NAS Miramar, CA
VF-96 'Fighting Falcons'	NAS Miramar, CA
VF-101 'Grim Reapers'	NAS Oceana, VA
VF-102 'Diamondbacks'	NAS Oceana, VA
VF-103 'Sluggers'	NAS Oceana, VA
VF-111 'Sundowners'	NAS Miramar, CA
VF-114 'Aardvarks'	NAS Miramar, CA
VF-121 'Pacemakers'	NAS Miramar, CA
VF-142 'Ghostriders'	NAS Miramar, CA
VF-143 'Pukin Dogs'	NAS Miramar, CA
VF-151 'Fighting Vigilantes'	NAF Atsugi, Japan
VF-154 'Black Knights'	NAS Miramar, CA
VF-161 'Chargers'	NAF Atsugi, Japan
VF-171 'Aces'	NAS Oceana, VA
VF-191 'Satan's Kittens'	NAS Miramar, CA
VF-194 'Hellfires'	NAS Miramar, CA
VF-201 'Rangers'	NAS Dallas, TX
VF-202 'Superheats'	NAS Dallas, TX
VF-213 'Black Lions'	NAS Miramar, CA

Squadron	Traditional home port
VF-301 'Devil's Disciples'	NAS Miramar, CA
VF-302 'Stallions'	NAS Miramar, CA
VAQ-33 'Hunters'	NAS Norfolk, VA
VX-4 'Evaluators'	NAS Point Mugu, CA

US Marine Corps

Squadron	Traditional base
VMFAT-101 'Sharpshooters'	MCAS Yuma, AZ
VMFA-112 'Wolf Pack'	NAS Dallas, TX
VMFA-115 'Silver Eagles'	VE MCAS Beaufort, SC
VMFA-122 'Crusaders'	MCAS Beaufort, SC
VMFAT-201	MCAS Cherry Point, NC
VMFA-212 'Lancers'	MCAS Kaneohe Bay, HI
VMFA-232 'Red Devils'	MCAS Iwakuni, Japan
VMFA-235 'Death Angels'	MCAS Kaneohe Bay, HI
VMFA-251 'Thunderbolts'	MCAS Beaufort, SC
VMFA-312 'Checkerboards'	MCAS Beaufort, SC
VMFA-314 'Black Knights'	MCAS El Toro, CA
VMFA-321 'Hell's Angels'	Andrews AFB, MD
VMFA-323 'Death Rattlers'	MCAS El Toro, CA
VMFA-333 'Shamrocks'	MCAS Beaufort, SC
VMFA-334 'Falcons'	MCAS El Toro, CA
VMFA-351	NAF Atlanta, GA
VMFA-451 'Warlords'	MCAS Beaufort, SC
VMFA-513 'Flying Nightmares'	MCAS El Toro, CA
VMFA-531 'Gray Ghosts'	MCAS Cherry Point, NC
VMFA-542 'Bengals'	MCAS El Toro, CA
VMCJ-1	MCAS Iwakuni, Japan
VMCJ-2 'Playboys'	MCAS Cherry Point, NC
VMCJ-3	MCAS El Toro, CA
VMFP-3 'Eyes of the Corps'	MCAS El Toro, CA

Appendix 5. Model Kits

Airfix

Aircraft	Scale
F-4E	1:144
F-4J/C/D/E	1:72

AMT/Ertl

Aircraft	Scale
F-4G Wild Weasel	1:48

Dragon

Aircraft	Scale
F-4E with revetment	1:144
F-4E 30th Anniversary	1:144
F-4S VF-151 'Switch Boxes'	1:144

Esci

Aircraft	Scale
F-4E	1:144
F-4E	1:48
F-4B/J	1:48
F-4C/D	1:48
F-4E Nam Raider	1:48
F-4 Black Bunny	1:48
F-4E/F	1:72
RF-4C/E Recce	1:72
F-4C/J	1:72
F-4E	1:72
F-4D Oregon ANG Egypt	1:72
RF-4C Desert Storm	1:72

Fujimi

Aircraft	Scale
F-4S Rockriver	1:72
F-4C/D Wolf Pack	1:72
F-4N Vigilantes	1:72
F-4EJ JASDF	1:72
F-4E USAF Mustang 01	1:72
F-4G Wild Weasel	1:72
F-4F West German	1:72
F-4E Thunderbirds	1:72
F-4J	1:72
F-4J Blue Angels	1:72
F-4B Jolly Rogers	1:72
F-4E MiG Killer	1:72
RF-4B	1:72
RF-4C Shogun	1:72
RF-4E JASDF	1:72
RF-4E Immelmann	1:72
F-4E 30th anniversary	1:72
F-4EJ	1:72
F-4K RN	1:72
F-4M Shark Teeth	1:72
F-4K Yellow	1:72
F-4E	1:48
F-4EJ	1:48
F-4E Thunderbirds	1:48
F-4D	1:72
F-4C/D/J	1:72
F-4E/EJ	1:72
RF-4C/E Japan Recce	1:72
F-4B/N Navy	1:72
F-4E/F	1:72
RF-4B/E Recce	1:72

Hasegawa

Aircraft	Scale
F-4EJ JASDF '99 competition	1:72
F-4S VMFA-321	1:72
F-4C/F MiG Killer	1:72
F-4B/N VF-51 CAG Screaming Eagles, Coral Sea	1:72
F-4E 5,000th Phantom	1:72
F-4EJ Kai Super Phantom	1:72
F-4E Bicentennial Bitburg	1:72
F-4F JG71 Special	1:72
YF-4E Edwards AFB	1:72
F-4E Israeli AF	1:72
F-4E	1:72
F-4S Vandy 75	1:72
F-4B/N Sundowners	1:72
F-4N Jolly Rogers	1:72
QF-4N Drone	1:48
F-4J VX-4 Vandy 76	1:48
F-4E Bicentennial '76	1:48
F-4S VMFA-321	1:48
F-4EJ Kai Super Phantom Black	1:48
F-4E Sharkmouth	1:48
F-4F JG71 Special	1:48
F-4E Thunderbirds	1:48
F-4J Blue Angels	1:48
F-4E 5,000th	1:48
F-4EJ JASDF	1:72
F-4E with Slats & TISEO	1:72
F-4F German	1:72
F-4J VX-4 Vandy	1:48
F-4F	1:72
F-4J	1:72
F-4S VF-151, VF-161, VMFA-235	1:72
F-4B/N VF-111, VF-151, VMFA-115	1:72
F-4C	1:72
F-4D 307TFS, Minnesota/New York ANG	1:72
F-4E 3TFW, New Jersey/Missouri ANG	1:72
F-4EJ JASDF	1:72
F-4G 52TFW	1:72
RF-4B	1:72
RF-4C USAF, ANG 38TRS, 15TRS, Alabama ANG	1:72
RF-4E JASDF, AG51, AG52	1:72
F-4EJ KAI Super 94 Air Competition	1:72
RF-4E Combat Competition	1:72

Hasegawa

Aircraft	Scale
F-4EJ Kai Super Phantom Gunnery Meet '95 306/302 Sqn	1:72
F-4J Black Bunny	1:72
F-4EJ Kai Super Phantom Gunnery Meet '95 301 Sqn	1:72
F-4EJ Kai ADTW 40th Anniversary	1:72
F-4C/D	1:72
F-4J/S	1:72
F-4B/N	1:72
F-4EJ	1:72
F-4G	1:48
F-4EJ Dragon Sqn	1:48
F-4E USAF Bataan	1:48
F-4G USAF Wild Weasel	1:48
F-4B/N USN	1:48
F-4C/D	1:48
F-4F West German	1:48
F-4EJ	1:48
F-4J Show Time 100	1:48
F-4EJ Kai Super Phantom	1:48
F-4E 30 Years Of Phabulous Phantoms	1:48
F-4G Wild Weasel	1:48
F-4B/N	1:48
F-4C/D Egypt I	1:48
F-4J Blue Angels	1:72
F-4E Thunderbird	1:72
JASDF F-4EJ EJ-KAI	1:72
F-4EJ Kai 1992 Gunnery Meet	1:72

Hobbycraft

Aircraft	Scale
F-4E USAF/Egypt	1:144
F-4E	1:144
F-4E	1:72
F-4F	1:72

Italeri

Aircraft	Scale
RF-4C	1:72
F-4E/G Wild Weasel	1:72
F-4S	1:72
RF-4C	1:48
F-4S USN	1:48
F-4E/F	1:48

LS

Aircraft	Scale
F-4E	1:144
F-4EJ	1:144
F-4F West Germany	1:144

Matchbox

Aircraft	Scale
F-4E Greek Air Force	1:72
F-4K/M	1:72
F-4K/M	1:72

Monogram

Aircraft	Scale
F-4	1:72
F-4E 30 Years Of Phabulous Phantoms	1:32
F-4J	1:72

Monogram

Aircraft	Scale
F-4C/D	1:72
F-4J	1:72
F-4J VX-4	1:48
F-4J VF-96	1:48
F-4C/D	1:48
F-4C/D	1:48

Tamiya

Aircraft	Scale
F-4C/D	1:32
F-4J	1:32
F-4J Marines	1:32
F-4E early	1:32

Revell

Aircraft	Scale
RF-4C	1:32
F-4F	1:32
F-4E/J	1:144
F-4F	1:72
RF-4E	1:72
RF-4E Luftwaffe	1:72
F-4B	1:72
F-4F	1:48
F-4F	1:72
RF-4C	1:32
F-4J and MiG-21 Double Set	1:48
RF-4E Tigermeet	1:32

Information on the model kits was supplied by H. G. Hannant Ltd: www.hannants.co.uk

Appendix 6. Further Reading

The Five Grand Fighter: McDonnell's Masterpiece Pt. II Air International, December 1978

Israel's Air Force: the Air War in the Mid East. Born In Battle No. 2 Eshel-Dramit Ltd, Israel, 1978

McDonnell Douglas F-4 Phantom II by Robert F. Dorr, Osprey Publishing London, 1984

McDonnell Douglas Aircraft since 1920 Volume II by Réne J. Francillon, Putnam London, 1990

Phantom In Combat by Walter J. Boyne, Schiffer Military/Aviation History, Atglen PA, 1994

Phantom: A Legend in Its Own Time by Francis K. Mason, PSL, 1984

F-4 Phantom by Bill Gunston, Charles Scribners Sons, New York, 1977

The Linebacker Raids: The Bombing of North Vietnam, 1972 by John T. Smith, Cassell & Co London, 2000

The F-4 Phantom II by G. G. O'Rourke, Arco Publishing Co Inc. USA, 1999

The F-4 Phantom II by Richard E. Gardner, Almarks Co Inc USA, 1970

The F-4 Phantom II (Parts 1 and 2) by R. Ward and Réne J. Francillon, Osprey Publications Ltd London, 1973

McDonnell Douglas F-4K and F-4M Phantom II by Michael Burns, Osprey Publishing Ltd London, 1984

Report MDC A2257 (Phantom II) McDonnell Aircraft Company, St Louis, 1973

...And Kill MiGs by L. Drendel, Squadron/Signal Publications, Texas USA, 1974

Projectair/Phantom II (Parts 1 & 2) J. Dewar Publications, Scotland, 1975

Configuration Studies, F/RF-4 Phantom McDonnell Aircraft Company, St Louis, 1976

The United States Air National by Guard Réne J. Francillon, Aerospace Publishing Limited, London/AIRtime Publishing, USA, 1993

American Combat Planes by Ray Wagner, Doubleday & Company, Garden City, New York, 1982

War In Peace: An Analysis of Warfare from 1945 to the Present Day Cons. Editor Sir Robert Thompson, Black Cat, 1988

Fighter Pilot: Aerial Combat Aces from 1914 to the Present Day edited by Brig-Gen Stanley M. Ulanoff, Prentice Hall Press, New York, 1986

Watch Out for Flying Weasels! by CMSgt Vickie M. Graham, Airman Magazine, April 1995

Air Force Magazine USAF Almanac 1991, 1994, and 1996

Cold Warriors and Desert Storm: USAFE In the Persian Gulf War by Thomas W. Thompson, Office of History HQ USAFE, 1994

United States Air Forces in Europe Historical Highlights 1942–1992 HQ USAFE 1993

United States Air Force Yearbook 1991 RAF Benevolent Fund International Air Tattoo Publishing Unit, 1991

Aircraft of the Vietnam War by Bill Gunston, PSL, Wellingborough, Northants, 1987

Vietnam: The War in the Air by Réne J. Francillon, Arch Cape Press, New York, 1987

The USAF At War, From Pearl Harbor to the Present Day by Martin W. Bowman, PSL, 1995

The World's Fastest Aircraft by Martin W. Bowman, PSL Wellingborough, Northants, 1990

Sunset for the Phantom by Bob Archer, Royal Air Force Yearbook, 1992

Phantom II, A Pictorial History by L. Drendel Squadron/Signal Publications, Texas USA, 1977

International Phantoms McDonnell Aircraft Company, St Louis, 1980

F-4 Phantom II (Parts 1, 2, & 3) by Bert Kinzey, Kalmbach K Books

US Navy F-4 Phantoms Pt I Atlantic Coast Markings by Bert Kinzey & Ray Leader, TAB Books Blue Ridge Summit, PA

US Navy F-4 Phantoms Pt II Pacific Coast Markings by Bert Kinzey & Ray Leader, Kalmbach K Books

Colors & Markings MiG Kill Markings From the Vietnam War Pt 1 USAF Aircraft by Bert Kinzey & Ray Leader, TAB Books Blue Ridge Summit, PA

Colors & Markings of the F-4E Phantom II C&M Vol. 13 Post Vietnam Markings by Bert Kinzey & Ray Leader, TAB Books Blue Ridge Summit, PA

Colors & Markings of the F-4D Phantom II C&M Vol. 4 Post Vietnam Markings by Bert Kinzey, TAB Books Blue Ridge Summit, PA

F-4C, F-4D & RF-4C Phantom II in detail & scale D&S Vol. 43 by Bert Kinzey, Kalmbach K Books

One Day in a Long War: May 10 1972 Air war North Vietnam by Jeffrey Ethell and Alfred Price, Greenhill, 1990

The Phantom Story by Anthony M. Thornborough and Peter E. Davies, Arms & Armour, 1994

McDonnell F-4 Phantom: Spirit in the Skies edited by Jon Lake, Aerospace Publishing Limited, London/AIRtime Publishing, USA, 1992

Index